Note all the logs in this aerial view of the shipyard in the late 1940s.

A HISTORY OF COLONNA'S SHIPYARD
and
ITS PEOPLE
1875–2011

A HISTORY OF COLONNA'S SHIPYARD
and
ITS PEOPLE
1875–2011

Raymond L. Harper

THE
DONNING COMPANY
PUBLISHERS

Copyright © 2012 by Colonna's Shipyard, Inc.
400 East Indian River Road
Norfolk, VA 23523

All rights reserved, including the right to reproduce this work in any form whatsoever without permission in writing from the publisher, except for brief passages in connection with a review. For information, please write:

The Donning Company Publishers
184 Business Park Drive, Suite 206
Virginia Beach, VA 23462

Steve Mull, *General Manager*
Barbara B. Buchanan, *Office Manager*
Richard A. Horwege, *Senior Editor*
Brett Oliver, *Graphic Designer*
Priscilla Odango, *Imaging Artist*
Lori Porter, *Project Research Coordinator*
Tonya Washam, *Marketing Specialist*
Pamela Engelhard, *Marketing Advisor*

Dennis N. Walton, *Project Director*

Library of Congress Cataloging-in-Publication Data

Harper, Raymond L.
    A history of Colonna's Shipyard and its people 1875–2011 / Raymond L. Harper.
        p. cm.
    Includes bibliographical references and index.
    ISBN 978-1-57864-741-5 (hbk. : alk. paper)
1. Colonna's Shipyard—History. 2. Colonna family. 3. Shipyards—Virginia—Norfolk—History.
4. Norfolk (Va.)—History, Naval. 5. Norfolk (Va.)—Biography. I. Title.
    VM299.6.H365 2012
    623.8'309755521—dc23

                                                        2012008116

Printed in the USA at Walsworth Publishing Company

CONTENTS

6 **Foreword** by W. W. Colonna Jr., Chairman of the Board of Colonna's Shipyard

9 **Preface**

13 **Introduction**

20 **Chapter I:** 1625–1900

50 **Chapter II:** 1900–1925

68 **Chapter III:** 1925–1955

82 **Chapter IV:** 1955–1980

94 **Chapter V:** 1980–2000

108 **Chapter VI:** 2000–2011

128 **Chapter VII:** Colonna's People

148 **Chapter VIII:** Employee's Activities and Benefits

162 **Chapter IX:** Breathtaking Point of Land

176 **Chapter X:** Tales of Old Berkley

184 **Bibliography**

186 **Index**

192 **About the Author**

FOREWORD

February 2011

Welcome to *A History of Colonna's Shipyard and Its People*—a message from Bill Colonna, past president, present owner, and chairman of the Board of Directors.

In 1875, just ten years after the War Between the States, my grandfather, Charles Jones Colonna, a twenty-six-year-old ship carpenter, designed and built his shipyard on a small parcel of leased property on the west side of what is now South Main Street in the Berkley section of the city of Norfolk.

Charles J. Colonna in later years.

Times were hard and money was scarce. Although feelings of division were still strong, the struggle between the North and the South had ended and a reunited nation had begun an era of growth never before realized. The port of Norfolk was busy and full of vessels of all kinds. Most of them were wooden and were powered by sail. All of those boats would at some time, need repairs. So with all those vessels finding their way into the Elizabeth River, Charles found himself in the midst of a thriving seaport, and with hard work and the proper equipment there was every opportunity to succeed.

Colonna's Shipyard has a long, interesting, and admirable history and is the second-oldest continuously family-owned-and-operated private shipyard in the United States. We often forget just how old this shipyard is and how conditions were in the early years. For many years most of the workforce either walked to work or rode their horses; hitching post and water buckets were provided at the shipyard. Also, a few kerosene lanterns were kept on hand to use for nighttime work. The shipyard has existed in three different centuries; the last quarter of the 1800s, all of the

Foreword

This image of the F/V Charles J. Colonna *was taken from a painting by Casey Holtzinger.*

1900s, and now well into the 2000s. During those years, ships powered by sail, steam, diesel, and nuclear as well as those constructed of wood, steel, aluminum, and fiberglass have received repairs or service at Colonna's.

For 136 years, one generation of the Colonna family after another has left its mark on the shipyard. My grandfather retired from the business in 1912. After that my father Will, Uncle Ben, and my cousin Ben Jr. led the shipyard. Then in 1977, it became my turn and today the yard is under the capable leadership of Tom Godfrey Jr.

With all of the improvements that have been accomplished in the past years, the shipyard still has a long way to go to be fully developed. I sincerely hope that the younger upcoming generations will follow the pattern set by earlier members of the family and continue to make improvements that will make Colonna's the best medium-size shipyard possible.

The shipyard management and office force today is excellent. Over a period of time the shipyard has been able to place the right people in the right positions. I think we have assembled the finest group of well-qualified professionals you could have.

The rank-and-file men and women who work in the shipyard trades are a pretty rugged group of individuals. They often work cold and rainy days in the winter and extremely hot days in summer. This is not easy work and only done by people with a certain strength of character. Sometimes when the workday is over and as they head out the gate in their wet and dirty clothes one could easily think that they are a bunch of nonskilled "red necks." In all fairness, maybe some of them are, however, for the most part they are the most skilled and talented people in the industry. They are members of that small group of Americans who still work with their hands, get dirty, cold, sweat, and leave the job each day with a feeling of pride and accomplishment for a job well-done.

As I look to the future of the shipyard, in my opinion, the greatest threats are over taxation and unnecessary rules, regulations, restrictions, and the national inclination toward socialism. These kill one's incentives and stifle growth.

In summary, I think the shipyard is just the most interesting place in the world, I always have. It has always been a challenge and not always easy, but the variety of work and interesting people make you want to come to work each day. The shipyard is large enough to make a statement, but not so big that it loses its individual identity. We have a close-knit working relationship with our employees, customers, business associates, and treat everyone fairly; a long and interesting history that few other companies have, and I think, a great sense of pride and accomplishment of a job well done.

As for me, I'll probably end up like my father who was born and lived his early years at the shipyard homestead, was president for forty-seven years, and then became chairman of the Board of Directors. When asked at the age of ninety-four what it felt like to be retired, his answer was, "Who the hell is retired?" I would like to thank everyone who works here or has ever worked here, for helping build the shipyard little by little, piece by piece. Many thanks and let's see if we can keep it going for at least another 136 years.

May 2011

At this time I have begun to turn the ownership and responsibility of the shipyard over to the younger generations.

W. W. Colonna Jr.,
Chairman of the Board

PREFACE

It was in early May 2008, that I received a phone call from W. W. Colonna Jr. Bill and I had known each other for several years and we both shared an interest in local history. He wanted to know if I had six copies of my new book, *A History of Chesapeake, Virginia*. When my answer was yes, he asked if I could visit him at the shipyard and bring the copies with me. One by one he called his granddaughters to his office, and I signed a book for each of them. Bill then asked if I would learn the operation of the shipyard and write its history. He figured it would take about three years to complete. At first, because of my age, the time involved, my doubts about being able to satisfactorily complete an assignment of this size and other commitments, I declined. I told Bill that I did not want to undertake the task because I was afraid that I might disappoint him. Being the gracious man that he usually is, his reply was, "I know you will not disappoint me." As you can see, after a considerable amount of encouragement, I finally agreed to give it a try.

The first step of what would prove to be a long journey toward writing this history was a trip to the Eastern Shore of Virginia to see where the Colonna family migrated upon leaving their home in Ireland. On June 3, 2008, Bill and his wife Evelyn and my wife Emma and I departed the shipyard and traveled to the Eastern

The Susan Constant, *a re-creation of one of the three ships that brought English colonists to Virginia in 1607, is usually moored at Jamestown Settlement's pier for visitors to explore. It was in Colonna's Shipyard for repair in March 1961.*

Shore where we spent most of the day exploring the areas around Accomack, the former community of Pennyville, and Pungoteague, Virginia. It was that time of year when tomato plants were being transplanted by the thousands and because of that and the muddy land we were unable to visit the Colonna family cemetery as planned.

Colonna's Shipyard, located in the Berkley section of Norfolk, Virginia, is the second-oldest continuously family-owned-and-operated private shipyard in the United States. The oldest being that of the Smith Brothers in Poquoson, Virginia. Colonna's Shipyard was established by Charles Jones Colonna in 1875. His original policy was "hard work, good value, and fair dealing," which he believed were the essentials necessary to earn the trust and respect of the customer. That original policy has served the company well for 136 years.

Recordkeeping has been an important part of the shipyard since its early years, and there was a plentiful supply of historical material available. However, much of it has not been cataloged, a problem that we hope to eventually correct. An archive that has been included on the third floor of the new office building, which was completed in late 2008, will provide space for most of the shipyard's historical records, photographs, and drawings.

On Sunday March 1, 1903, Benjamin Azariah (az-uh-ri-uh) Colonna, brother of Charles Jones Colonna, began writing volume one of his autobiography. Years later, between 1941 and 1945, his daughter Eileen Alton Colonna Mitchell along with her niece, Lucy Brisebois, read over Benjamin's collection of papers, letters, journals, and accounts with the intent of finishing what he had started earlier in the century. While in her twenties Eileen had begun typing her father's work and now, later in life, picking up where she left off, Eileen continued until her eyes began to fail and she was unable to finish the project. At that time her daughter Ellen Britton undertook the task, which when complete, amounted to two volumes. Lucy Brisebois also contributed to the task of typing the original manuscript, then had it printed and passed out copies at the first Colonna's Shipyard reunion in 1984. It was soon updated and duplicated by Virginia (Jinx) Mansfield Colonna and distributed to members of the family at the next Colonna reunion that was held in the Oaklette section of the Washington borough of Chesapeake, Virginia, in 1985. Those two well-written volumes contributed a sizable amount of valuable information about the formative years of the shipyard.

In July 1988, Bill Colonna completed volume one of his "Colonna Papers" and in May 1996, he finished volume two. Also in the latter 1980s before I retired from my career in federal service and began writing local history, a gentleman by the name of John Frey began writing a history of Colonna's Shipyard. In 1990, when the corporation went into bankruptcy, Mr. Frey was directed to discontinue writing its history. Afterwards he relocated to the mountains of Virginia and is now deceased.

All of the above documents contain important information about the history of Colonna's Shipyard and some of the information from each has been included in this book. Other sources include many on-site visits to the shipyard, where Bill and I walked the fifty-plus acres to include the dry docks where we walked beneath large ships; upon looking up at the ship's bottoms I thought if they fell we both would be crushed like a couple of bugs.

Other information used in this history include material from the archives of the Preston Library at the Virginia Military Institute in Lexington, Virginia; papers presented by the Society of Naval Architects and Marine Engineers; articles from *The Colonna Pilot* and the Norfolk newspapers; research from the history room of the Norfolk Central Library; the office of the Clerk of the Circuit Court in Chesapeake, Virginia; the Clerk's Office of the Circuit Court of Northampton County, Virginia; both of my histories of Chesapeake, Virginia; the many file folders, scrapbooks, and photo albums found in the archives at Colonna's Shipyard; the letters, journals, diaries, and private account books of Benjamin Azariah Colonna; letters written by his sons Benjamin Allison Colonna and Colonel John Owen Colonna; and the valuable information written by the late Nicholas W. Paxson, who worked at Colonna's Shipyard for forty-five years, retiring as vice president of the corporation.

During my tenure at Colonna's Shipyard I was privileged to participate in many interviews with W. W. Colonna Jr., the current owner. And from those interviews several topics of historical importance were gleaned. The following three, "Early

Nicholas W. Paxson retired as vice president of the corporation after forty-five years at Colonna's Shipyard.

years in the Shipyard," "Shipyard Threats," and a group of lighthearted "Tales of Old Berkley," have been included in great detail.

Photographs of the first shipyard were not available; however, using information obtained from the archives and possibly adding a little imagination, Manfred W. "Casey" Holtzinger, a local artist was able to produce accurate paintings of Charles J. Colonna's first ship repair facility on the Eastern Branch of the Elizabeth River. Eventually Casey was commissioned to paint forty pictures of ships and structures owned by Colonna's Shipyard as well as early churches of the nearby community of Berkley. Casey often commented that those forty paintings were among the best that he had ever done because so much research and knowledge of subject matter was required to complete each one of them. Because of the research involved he acquired a deep personal interest in each painting. The entire collection along with information sheets and signed releases has been placed on the Internet in order that others may use and enjoy them.

Many photographs that appear in this book were taken by Don Beecham of Virginia Beach, Virginia. The aerial photographs were produced by Backus Aerial Photography of Chesapeake, Virginia. Others were taken by W. W. Colonna Jr., his daughter Karen, and possibly other members of the shipyard family. Most of the very early photographs were found on file in the archives on the third floor of the office building.

Since *A History of Colonna's Shipyard and Its People* covers such a large number of years, I felt that for the most part it would be advantageous to use periods of time as chapter titles, for example, "Chapter I, 1625–1900," "Chapter II, 1900–1925," etc. However, in some cases it has been necessary to use other types of titling.

I would like to add that my time spent at Colonna's Shipyard was one of the highlights of my life. I found the people to be pleasant and always willing to lend a helping hand. I was able to interview a cross-section of the employees as well as some members of the Board of Directors; however, I regret that it was not possible for me to spend time with every worker employed at what I consider to be the best-kept secret in the Maritime Industry. Thanks folks for all your help. It is to Colonna's people that I dedicate this story.

Please note that in the early chapters the designation "Sr." is missing from Captains Carl, Will, and Ben Colonna's names; however, after their sons were born the designation was added to distinguish between the senior and junior member of each family.

INTRODUCTION

It is not certain exactly where the Colonna family originated before settling in Ireland. Occasionally, we hear stories about them being related to the Colonna family of Italy, but no concrete evidence has been found to prove that they originated from that part of the world. It seems, however, that they were quite adaptive at traveling large distances in search of better living conditions; for we have been able to determine that they were among the earliest settlers of Virginia. The belief is that the early family members came to America from Dublin, Ireland, during the Irish Civil War. The first known record of a family member is the will of "Owen Collony," which is dated the year 1666 and can be found in the Accomack County, Virginia Courthouse. Before the year 1835 there were several spellings of the family name; it was at that time a meeting was held and a decision was made that the official name, from that day forward, would be "Colonna."

At the time of this writing the Colonna family consists of eleven generations; however, our history will not cover all of them, but will begin with the sixth generation of which John Watson Colonna (1805–1871) was a part. He was the father of eight children, two of whom played important roles in the establishment of Colonna's Shipyard. Prior to and during the War Between the States, John Watson Colonna was a prominent businessman and successful farmer on the Eastern Shore of Virginia. He also, along with the assistance of other members of the family, operated four sailing vessels.

In 1836, John Watson Colonna married Sarah Boggs, a native of Accomack County. Their son, John Thomas, was born in 1840 and his mother died the following year. In 1842, John Watson married second, Margaret Jones (1818–1856) of New York. Margaret was a descendant of a long line of shipbuilders.

John Watson and Margaret Jones became the parents of seven children, which included: Benjamin Azariah (1843–1924), Elizabeth Esther (1845–1945), Sarah Cornelia (1847–1870), Charles Jones (1849–1920), Major Duncan (1852–unknown), Rebecca Robb (1854–1863), and a baby boy that was still born December 29, 1856. Margaret Jones Colonna died the next day.

On October 17, 1843, Benjamin Azariah Colonna (also remembered as Ben or BAC) was born at the homestead near Pungoteague in Accomack County, Virginia. He was the first son of John Watson and Margaret Jones Colonna. At that time, his father was serving as a first mate in the steamboat service between Baltimore,

The US Coast Guard's Legare 912 *on marine railway No. 4 in 1993.*

Maryland, and the Eastern Shore of Virginia. One year later in 1844, John Watson was made captain of the steamboat *Frick*. Almost six years after Ben was born, on August 28, 1849, his younger brother Charles Jones Colonna was born in the same house and in the same room where Benjamin had been born.

Benjamin was the only member of his immediate family to receive an advanced education. He wanted very much to attend the Virginia Military Institute (VMI) at Lexington, Virginia. He applied for and was granted a scholarship as a state cadet to VMI; however, his father still had to pay a portion of his tuition. In 1859, John Watson Colonna scraped together every cent he possibly could in order that his son Benjamin could receive a college education. In doing so he told Ben that after his graduation from VMI he expected him to be responsible for his brothers and sisters. Ben agreed and took that responsibility seriously for the rest of his life.

Benjamin A. Colonna and the other cadets at VMI were called upon to fight at the battle of New Market, Virginia, during the War Between the States. Upon graduation he became a captain in the Army of the Confederate States of America.

On May 11, 1864, Benjamin's half brother John Thomas Colonna was shot to death along with several other young Confederate soldiers. They had just been captured and were sitting on a fence at the homestead of the Vaughn family in Gloucester County, Virginia. Thinking they were spies, Commander Draper of the Massachusetts Colored Regiment, gave the order to shoot them. John Thomas and the others were buried on Captain Vaughn's property.

After the war Benjamin became a schoolteacher in Accomack County where he taught his younger brothers Charles and Major and other area students. He held classes in a one-room house that was situated behind the Accomack County Courthouse on the back part of the lot. Growing weary of teaching and seeking more profitable employment, in the summer of 1870, Ben began working for the United States Coast and Geodetic Survey.

In his childhood and youth Charles J. Colonna worked on his father's farm and attended the county free schools. When he was about eighteen years of age he went to Chicago, Illinois, served an apprenticeship as a ship carpenter and then took up the life offered by the sea.

In 1870 Charles hired on as ship carpenter on the CSS *Bibb*, a Coast and Geodetic Survey ship, which was a side-wheel coast survey steamer with sails. Soon afterwards the ship, being in need of service, pulled into the shipyard of William A. Graves Sr. on the Eastern Branch of the Elizabeth River in Norfolk, Virginia. While there, Charles heard that Graves was in need of a ship carpenter so he approached him and inquired about the possibility of employment. Charles was hired and worked about two years at Graves Shipyard. Around 1875 things were not going well at the shipyard; and for some time Charles' brother Benjamin had been trying to encourage him to enter into business for himself. After giving it some thought, Charles resigned his position at the Graves' Shipyard, leased property from the Hardy family across the river in Norfolk County (later Berkley) and took the first steps that would eventually lead to a successful shipyard business.

Money, as it often is, was in short supply so Charles began his business in 1875 by performing repairs on pier-side ship decks, superstructures, and interiors. It was in the final days of commercial sailing vessels in America, and the era of the windjammers and their thirty thousand square yards of rigging were swiftly coming to an end. Early invoices and letterheads listed the original name of the business as "Chas. J. Colonna—Shipwright, Spar Maker and Caulker."

By all indications it appears that two years after beginning his business, Charles added his first marine railway. An entry in his brother Benjamin's journal dated February 15, 1877, reported that Charles had built a marine railway. At that time Benjamin was in Washington, D.C., awaiting orders to San Francisco, California, and was able to take the steamboat *Lady of the Lake* to Norfolk to see the operation firsthand. The lifting capacity of this first marine railway was about forty tons. The name of the business then became known as "Chas. J. Colonna's Marine Railway."

Throughout the years there would be several other name changes. After acquiring a second railway the name became "Chas. J. Colonna Marine Railways." In 1882, it became Colonna Dry-Dock and Shipbuilding Company. Then on March 30, 1907, the business was incorporated and became known as Colonna Marine Railway, Corporation. Judge William N. Portlock of the Circuit Court of Norfolk County signed the certificate of incorporation. On December 31, 1921, Colonna Marine Railway, Corporation, and Marine Iron Works merged under the name of Colonna's Shipyard, Inc., and has done business under that name ever since.

The slipways, later known as marine railways, using the principle of the inclined plane to remove ships from the water, had its beginning in North America around 1840. It was originally conceived as a launch way operating in reverse with primitive greased ways providing the low friction interface between the sliding cradle and the ground ways. The first marine railways were powered by horsepower. Depending upon the size of the vessel, one or two real horses, attached to a turnstile were used to pull it out of the water. Around 1900, the horses were retired and power was obtain from steam engines and years later the shipyards graduated to the use of large gears and chains operated by electric motors.

Ben having pledged his future support to his brothers and sisters was especially faithful to his brother Charles in his attempt to build a successful shipyard business. He was faithful to the point that he helped him financially to acquire land necessary to build a bigger and better shipyard.

Even with the assistance of his brother, Charles found the going very hard at times; on several occasions he said the shipyard business was too hard and he could see no future in it. Had it not been for the encouragement offered by his wife Margaret it is almost certain that he would have given up all hope of ever fulfilling his dream of developing a successful shipyard. As we will see later, throughout the history of Colonna's Shipyard, some of the ladies played an important role in the successes of the business. Remember, as the old adage goes, "Behind every successful man there is a good and faithful woman."

As Colonna's Shipyard grew its primary products were wooden hull vessels such as pilot boats, side-wheel riverboats, and menhaden fishing vessels. Captain Will Colonna, son of Charles Jones Colonna, saw the shipbuilding industry graduate from sail to steam to diesel and then to nuclear power. The last five-mast schooner to dock at Colonna's Shipyard was in the year 1937. Today's shipyard is a full facility yard that is equipped to service most all maritime requirements including inside and outside machine work, electric, carpenter, paint and sandblasting, docking, ship fitting, pipefitting, and engine servicing.

As stated above, the establishment has certainly had its share of difficulties. Throughout the years, local bank loans have been the norm for operating and improvement funds; however, even with borrowed money, in 1990 a bad contract with the US government forced the corporation into Chapter 11 bankruptcy. Although by November 1992, conditions had begun to improve and the business was well on the road to recovery. Since that time there have been many major improvements in the operation.

Today, when driving along East Indian River Road, a short distance west of Wilson Road and past the Riverside Cemetery, one can see a new addition to the skyline. There towering above all the other shipyard buildings is the new three-story office complex with the Colonna emblem at the top. At first glance it may seem out of place standing there among the everyday hustle and bustle of a busy shipyard. I can just imagine that past generations would be proud of this new structure that now stands where many years ago Benjamin A. Colonna planted a row of Ginkgo trees. The last tree was removed in order to construct this much-needed building.

A short distance from the new office building and across Pescara Creek is the West Yard where phase one of a three-phase development was begun in 2008.

At the time of this writing (2011) Colonna's Shipyard has two marine railways, Nos. 3 and 4, and two floating dry docks. Colonna's full-service team includes the divisions of Steel America, Flow Control Technologies, Down River, and Colonna Yachts. Among its subsidiaries are Trade Team, Norfolk Barge, and Ocean Tech. The current owner of Colonna's Shipyard, Inc., is Willoughby Warren Colonna Jr., a member of the ninth generation of the family.

In its many years of operation the shipyard has had six names and also six presidents and chief executive officers (CEOs).

The shipyard names past and present:

- (1875) Chas. Colonna—Shipwright, Spar Maker and Caulker
- (1877) Chas. J. Colonna's Marine Railway
- (1880) Chas. J. Colonna's Marine Railways
- (1882) Colonna Dry-Dock and Shipbuilding Company
- (March 30, 1907) Colonna Marine Railway, Corporation
- (December 31, 1921) Colonna's Shipyard, Inc.

The shipyard presidents and chief executive officers (CEOs):

- (1875–1907) Charles Jones Colonna, founder
- (1907–1954) Willoughby Warren Colonna Sr.
- (1954–1968) Benjamin Okeson Colonna Sr.
- (1968–1977) Benjamin Okeson Colonna Jr.
- (1977–1993) Willoughby Warren Colonna Jr.
- (1993–present) Thomas Walter Godfrey Jr.

The shipyard Board of Directors for the year 2011:

- W. W. Colonna Jr.—Chairman of the Board
- Carl M. Albero—Vice Chairman of the Board
- Thomas W. Godfrey Jr.—President and Chief Executive Officer (CEO)
- Waverly Berkley III—Secretary and Corporate Counsel
- John D. Pagett—Director
- VADM Jim Metzger, USN(Ret.)—Director
- Ronald Ward—Director
- Karen M. Colonna—Director
- Randall Crutchfield—Director

Introduction

Charles J. Colonna was founder and president and CEO of the shipyard from 1875 to 1907.

Willoughby Warren Colonna Sr. served as president and CEO of Colonna's Shipyard from 1907 to 1954.

Benjamin Oakeson Colonna Sr. became president and CEO of Colonna's Shipyard in 1954 and served until 1968.

Benjamin Oakeson Colonna Jr. followed his father as president and CEO of Colonna's Shipyard in 1968 and served in that position until 1977.

Willoughby Warren Colonna Jr. became president and CEO of Colonna's Shipyard in 1977 and served until 1993.

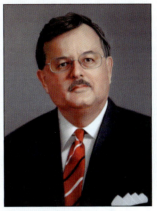

Thomas Walter Godfrey Jr. became president and CEO of Colonna's Shipyard in 1993 and is currently serving in that position.

Chapter I

1625–1900

The Early Family

The Eastern Shore of Virginia, that's where our story begins, for it was there that the Colonna family settled in 1661, or possibly as early as 1625. The will of the first member of the family in America, "Owen Collony," was recorded in the Accomack County Courthouse in 1666. In the earlier years of our country, most of the people had very little education and therefore whenever a name was written it was always spelled the way it sounded to the individual. Therefore, a family name could have an unlimited number of spellings. For example, the members of the first generation were known as *Collonie*, the second-generation name was *Collony*, and the third- and fourth-generation members were known as *Colony*.

The old Colonna home on the Eastern Shore of Virginia dates back to the 1600s or early 1700s. John Watson Colonna, father of Charles J. Colonna, acquired the home in 1853.

After several generations the family members had acquired more education and learned to read and write. So, in August 1835, Dr. Nicholas Sherar held a meeting in the yard of his residence on Nandua Creek near Pennysville for the purpose of adopting a common spelling of the family name. After deliberating all day and not reaching a decision the good doctor suggested that the family name become *Colonna*. A vote was taken and after a bit of a hassle, those present agreed to the new spelling of the family name.

John Watson Colonna, father of Benjamin Azariah and Charles Jones Colonna—the two members of the family who would eventually establish the Colonna Marine Railway—operated a general merchandise store and was a prominent farmer in the former community of Pennyville. He also owned and—with the assistance of other members of the family—operated four wooden sailing vessels before and during the War Between the States. Some of the fruits and vegetables grown on his farm were shipped to the ports along the Chesapeake Bay; however, most of the fruit was kept to make brandy, which could be used for trading and possibly medicinal purposes. Some of the vessels were used to carry pots and pans, iron implements, cloth, and other goods to the Bahamas where they could be traded for sugar, molasses, and rum that could be sold to ports along the Chesapeake Bay. Business was good but as we will see the War Between the States would leave John Watson penniless.

On December 30, 1856, John Watson's wife Margaret Jones died after having given birth to a stillborn baby boy the previous day. After her death John Watson's Aunt Peggy, in her old age, came to run the household.

The War Between the States wiped out most of the Colonna family's possessions and on March

This photo of John Watson Colonna, father of Charles J. Colonna, was taken in 1862.

12, 1866, John Watson Colonna signed a Deed of Trust to his oldest son Benjamin for the benefit of Edward C. Satchell and twenty-two other creditors. The total debt including interest was $1,600. Four years after all his father's possessions were sold; Benjamin set him up in the feed, grain, and seed business in Norfolk, Virginia. By 1870, John Watson Colonna was in a partnership with a Mr. Saunders. The two men were so busy that they were closely confined to the store. Their average business income was $100 per day.

Charles Jones Colonna

Charles Jones Colonna, having been born August 27, 1849, was six years younger than his brother Benjamin Azariah. In his childhood and youth Charles lived and worked on his father's farm just north of what was then the village of Pennyville near Pungoteague in Accomack County, Virginia. He attended the county free schools but, due to family finances, was unable to attend an institution of higher learning. When his formal education ceased he remained home until he was about eighteen years of age. In order to make a living the family became separated. Charles went to Chicago, Illinois, and served an apprenticeship as a ship carpenter. It was then that he took up the life offered by the sea. He sailed before the mast on the schooner *C.C. Sadler* for two years and then worked as a ship carpenter for the firm of Miller and Brothers. His trade also took him to other places such as Canada and Michigan. After sailing on several ships and even having experienced the horrors of being shipwrecked,

This circa 1889 photograph of Charles J. Colonna was taken when he was about forty years of age.

Charles went to Brooklyn, New York, and worked in the shipyard of Azariah Jones, which was owned by his mother's family.

CSS *Bibb*

In the early 1870s Charles was working as a ship carpenter on the *Bibb* a Coast and Geodetic Survey ship. The CSS *Bibb* was a coast side-wheel survey steamer with sails and was 160 feet in length. This was the second ship by the name *Bibb*. It had been launched at the Boston Navy Yard on May 12, 1853. The *Bibb* was transferred from the Coast Survey to the Revenue Cutter Service, a forerunner of the

In the early 1870s Charles J. Colonna was a ship carpenter on the CSS Bibb. *The* Bibb *was a Coast and Geodetic Survey side-wheel steamer that had been launched at the Boston Navy Yard on May 12, 1853.*

Coast Guard, in April 1861, but was returned to the Coast Survey in November of the same year. It later saw service with the Union forces. With return to peacetime conditions the *Bibb* resumed service with the Coast Survey.

The ship later sailed into an Elizabeth River pier near the southern end of Norfolk, Virginia, in the vicinity where Lord Dunmore's five ships had bombarded the town on January 1, 1776. The *Bibb* was soon pulled up a marine railway at the shipyard of William A. Graves Sr. There it would receive necessary repairs as well as its periodic overhaul, which included scraping barnacles and replacement of planks, beams, futtocks, and other timbers afflicted with rot. Necessary recalking and painting would also be accomplished at that time.

Graves and Bro. Shipwrights

Graves' Marine Railway was one of several along either side of the Elizabeth River and up into its Southern, Eastern, and Western Branches. Some had been a part of the history of Norfolk and Portsmouth. Graves started in business in 1851 and at that time was listed as "Graves and Bro. Shipwrights." The facility was

William A. Graves Sr. owned and operated Graves Shipyard and was affiliated with the Virginia Pilot Association. Charles J. Colonna was employed by Graves for about two years when he first came to Norfolk.

William A. Graves Jr. was general manager of his father's shipyard and inherited the business when his father died.

located at 66 East Widewater Street near present-day Town Point. W. A. Graves' Shipyard had helped repair Confederate ships during the War Between the States, and a few of the nearby shipyards could even lay claim to the building of ships used during the War of 1812.

Upon arrival of a ship, especially after bad weather, the ship carpenter was kept busy refitting the damaged vessel. When a ship limped up the Elizabeth River, any cargo she might have was unloaded, her sails and rigging stored in a nearby loft, and her crew was lodged at various local ordinaries. The ship was then hauled in for repairs. The ship's carpenter and the captain were probably the only two men aboard that knew what repairs a wooden vessel would need after a year or more at sea. The carpenter also knew that any repairs he could make himself would save money and reduce the amount of time in port. This additional effort was appreciated by the ship's owner as well as the captain and likely earned the carpenter their gratitude. As long as the ship's carpenter was busy with repairs he would not be going ashore, wasting his money and possibly getting into trouble. Norfolk was a seaport then as it is today. In earlier years it was filled with saloons, pimps, and prostitutes who were on the lookout for sailors that had been at sea for long periods of time and had accumulated a fair amount of cash.

While the *Bibb* was in W. A. Graves' Shipyard Charles heard through the grapevine that there was an opening for a good ship carpenter. Figuring "nothing ventured, nothing gained," he decided to ask Graves for a job. As luck would have it Mr. Graves did need a ship carpenter and gave the job to Charles J. Colonna. Charles signed off the *Bibb*, brought his tools ashore and found a room at a boarding house on Brewer Street near Charlotte Street in Norfolk, possibly the one operated by his sister Elizabeth.

His place of residence was within walking distance of the shipyard, which at that time was advertised as "W. A. Graves Marine Facility at 211 to 219 Water Street." The only available public transportation then was the city's horse-drawn streetcars and in the winter of 1872/73 there was an epidemic of horse influenza that put the streetcar company out of business. So it was good that he could walk to work. Also by walking that distance he was able to save the nickel fare that was normally charged by the streetcar company.

At some point around 1874 Charles and his boss William Graves had a disagreement of some kind. It is possible that Charles felt his chances of promotion were slim and that eventually Graves' son who was general manager would become owner of the business. Also, another member of the family, David Graves, was yard foreman.

Colonna's First Ship Repair Facility

It was about that time that Charles' brother Benjamin began to encourage him to select a suitable place for a modest shipyard and enter the small vessel repair business. With the intent of going into business for his self, Charles left the employ of William A. Graves and with a loan of $1,800 from his brother Benjamin, he leased property owned by Thomas Asbury Hardy across the river in what was then Norfolk County (In 1890 this area would become the town of Berkley). Attorney W. B. Martin of Norfolk drew up the terms of the agreement between the brothers. The location was on the west side of Main Street (later known as South Main Street) at the edge of the Elizabeth River directly across from the Hardy home (formerly the Herbert plantation). The land that he leased was in the vicinity of the foot ferry to Norfolk and near where the first steel bridge to Norfolk would be built in 1916.

With experience gained from his employment at Azariah Jones' shipyard in Brooklyn, New York; at Graves in Norfolk, Virginia; and having worked on a variety of vessels, Charles knew what was required in order to build a marine railway and shipyard. To begin with space was needed for the rails and platform to rise out of the water from navigable depths beyond the lowest tide—still at least a ship's length clear of the channel. He had seen how a northwest gale could drive water out of the Chesapeake Bay and lower normal low water levels, even pushing some water into the Elizabeth River which in turn caused many of the low-lying streets of Norfolk to flood.

Ashore the railway also needed adequate working space. The rails must extend on solid footing ashore far enough to accommodate several craft, whether they were watermen's workboats or ships. Then power had to be provided. Men alone could not be expected to turn winches heavy enough to pull as much as forty tons up the incline. While forty tons in water can be pushed by hand, out of water it becomes absolute dead weight. The means of moving the vessel here, as well as at Graves and many other railways, would be pure horsepower provided by real live horses, mules, or oxen.

The railway establishment would also require adequate storage space. Room was necessary for unseasoned lumber to be racked and air-dried for at least one

This painting by Casey Holtzinger is based on information from shipyard archives and depicts how Charles J. Colonna's first shipyard may have looked in the summer of 1875.

year. Sheds were needed for tools and other equipment. Stables had to be built for the horses. It was essential that the facility have a blacksmith shop and machine works shed to make or repair chainplates, cleats, shackles, sheaves, winders, and other metalwork, including boilers and engines of steam tugs. A woodworking shop was also a necessity for dressing rough lumber, cutting it to the proper dimensions, and making or repairing ship cabinets and furniture. These were the absolute essentials for the early business. As the establishment grew and became profitable other equipments and spaces would be added for such services as sail and spar making, rigging, painting, caulking, etc.

All of this would require money and would also take a considerable amount of time to build. Charles possibly had some savings from his wages at Graves but he also needed money to live on while building and equipping the facility. As previously mentioned, money was in short supply and before building the marine railway and shipyard he began his business by performing repairs on pier-side ship decks, superstructure, and interiors. The exact date of the initial operation of "Chas. J. Colonna's Marine Railway" is uncertain; however, information written by Benjamin in his journal dated February 15, 1877, reads, "During the fall & winter of 1876/77 my brother Charles has built a marine railway at Norfolk, Va. and his prospects of succeeding are well." Benjamin left Washington, D.C., for Norfolk on Tuesday February 20, 1877, on the steamer *Lady of the Lake* to see the yard firsthand. He spent five days visiting with Charles and returned to Washington, D.C., on Sunday, February 25, 1877. What Benjamin saw upon his arrival in Norfolk was a horse-drawn marine railway with a bed way type track, having a lifting capacity of about forty tons. It traveled on a system of free rollers having a diameter of four inches and a tread of four inches. These early rollers were relatively unstable and had considerable trouble remaining on the track.

So, just ten years after the War Between the States ended Charles Jones Colonna, then a twenty-six-year-old journeyman ship carpenter, designed and built this small marine railway and shipyard with a capacity of just forty tons. That was the largest job that he expected for a while. It was a desperate time for the South coming on the heels of the war. Money was scarce, but with all the hardships, it was still an exciting time for this young man. In spite of the recent horrors of war and the Reconstruction period that followed there was some semblance of unity in our country. The port was busy and literally full of vessels of all kinds, and all those boats, would at sometime, need repairs. Thus Charles J. Colonna found himself in the midst of a thriving seaport and with hard work there were many opportunities to succeed.

The first years of operation were very hard for young Colonna; although there was an abundance of work his railway was so limited that he could haul only small boats, and therefore his profits were very small. Had it not been for the help and constant encouragement offered by his wife Margaret Okeson Dunston whom he married in March 1877, Colonna possibly would have given up all hope and closed the business. However, in July of that year Charles wrote his brother Ben that the shipyard was busy and had all the work he could handle. There was a schooner on the railway and a sloop called the *Yankee* was waiting for a new keel. As time goes on we will see that some of the wives played an important role in the operation of what would become a lucrative shipyard business.

The question that may come to mind is, "Why didn't Mr. Colonna seek a loan or buy on credit?" Actually the first nearby Loan Company would not open until 1886 and there was no such thing as credit in those days. As we will see later there were some well-to-do people who might lend a financial helping hand. However, in spite of the dark clouds there were still a few things in his favor. There were numerous sawmills at nearby Washington Point. Some such as that of E. M. Tilley were operated by "Damn Yankees" that came south after the war, not only to make a few bucks, but also to help the southerners get on their feet. The operation of those mills meant that there was an unlimited supply of lumber of all sizes and kinds. There was also plenty of timber in the forests that covered much of the local area.

Boat lumber of the straightest grain came to the many steam-powered sawmills serving the local shipyards. Pine and oak could still be found in the local dense forests. A large number of logs, which were used for the manufacture of lumber, came from the forests and swamps of North Carolina, the neighboring counties of Virginia, and the Great Dismal Swamp. After the logs were harvested, they were usually floated through canals that connected to the Elizabeth River.

The Norfolk harbor was an extremely busy place as water transportation was cheap and dependable and took the place of our present-day transportation systems. Many places could not be reached by land travel. Most transport was by water; produce was brought by boat from the farms of Norfolk County and North Carolina to the markets of Norfolk. There was water taxi service from one point to another. In other words the rivers were the highways of those days. Most of the vessels were still made of wood and were powered by large stately sails. These included fish trawlers, oyster boats, barges, and bogies and their construction and repairs required the skills of ship carpenters, riggers, sail makers, wood caulkers, painters, and blacksmiths.

As previously mentioned, the first Colonna Marine Railway had a lifting capacity of forty tons. The cradle or carriage which had the hauling chain attached to the inshore end ran on four-inch-wide iron tracks with four-inch-diameter iron rollers. In order to pull a boat out of the water the cradle or carriage was lowered under the floating vessel. The railway rested on a mat of flat boards, which in turn rested on the graded inclined mud bottom. The boards being subjected to water eventually rotted or were destroyed by teredos (ship worms) and required periodic replacement. Because of this type of construction, the railway was commonly referred to as a "floored railway."

Depending on the size and weight of the vessel either one or two horses were required to pull it out of the water. The horses were harnessed to a cross arm that was attached to a vertical shaft or "kingpost" that was supported in a vertical

There being no photograph available, information from the archives and a little imagination were used by Casey Holtzinger to paint this scene of Charles J. Colonna's Marine Railway in the winter of 1875.

position. As the horses walked in a circle around the "kingpost" the force that they exerted through the cross arm caused the vertical shaft to turn; this force was transferred to a horizontal shaft by means of a pair of bevel gears, one of which was fixed to the lower end of the vertical shaft and mated with a corresponding gear that was fixed to one end of the horizontal shaft. At a point approximately midway of this shaft, a spur gear was fixed which in turn engaged a larger spur gear that was fixed to a shaft along with a chain sprocket and positioned to the rear of the main shaft. It was this sprocket that gripped the railway cradle hauling chain and as the shaft turned, the cradle, along with the vessel resting on its blocks, was drawn up the inclined plane of the tracks, and out of the water. To the other end of the horizontal shaft was fixed a brake drum with a manually operated brake band with screw clamping arrangement. This brake was not only used to secure the cradle in its uphaul position but it also aided in controlling the travel speed of the cradle as it rolled backward by gravitational force, into the water. This railway did not have a downhaul chain and the entire mechanism was located between the tracks at the inshore end.

This early horse-drawn turnstile was used at Charles J. Colonna's Marine Railway to pull small vessels out of the water.

The pier that extended from the shoreline to deep water was constructed of pile bents with a flat board decking about five feet wide. The offshore end of the pier was built in the shape of an "L." It was here that vessels waiting to be docked or waiting for repair were tied-up.

The buildings of the shipyard, which included the office building and various work sheds, were of wood frame construction with board and batten exterior. Everything was simply done; however, it was all Charles J. Colonna needed in the beginning. A year later he was able to purchase an advertisement in the Norfolk Directory. It actually appeared on the same page as the federal collector of Internal Revenue who had an office in the Custom House on Main Street and the Commissioner of the Revenue whose office was located in the Courthouse at the foot of City Hall Avenue where the MacArthur Memorial is today. Both buildings were located in the city of Norfolk, Virginia. The Colonna advertisement carried no telephone number because it would be 1879 before the phone company could offer service to fifty residents and businesses in Norfolk.

By this time Charles' brother Benjamin Azariah was working in California with the US Coast and Geodetic Survey. As often as he could manage Ben would send money to help Charles finance operation of the shipyard. The brothers had formed an informal partnership that would scare the pants off any businessman in today's world. The only existing records would be the letters and telegrams between two loyal and trusting brothers.

About mid-1880 Benjamin, knowing that Charles' lease from the Hardy family was nearing expiration and that his business had increased, wrote and advised him to look around for a suitable site to purchase for his railway. Benjamin also stated that he would, under suitable conditions, buy the land for him. With an eye on the future, he told Charles that it was important that he acquire property on a deepwater channel.

First Land Purchase

On August 23, 1880, Charles wrote his brother Benjamin about purchasing approximately thirty-seven acres known as the Hardy Farm. The property at that time was located between the Hardy place and the Norfolk and Western Railroad Bridge and was owned by N. B. Foreman. In his letter Charles asked Benjamin to send the sum of $2,000 as a down payment. On September 15, 1880, Benjamin wrote that he was in favor of the purchase, but would like a title search first, after which he would send the money. On the same day, Benjamin also wrote his attorney Lafayette Harmanson and asked him to perform a title search of the property. Two days later, Benjamin received another letter from Charles this time saying that he had signed an agreement on September 14, 1880, to purchase the property. After receiving that information, Benjamin felt obligated to send the first payment amounting to $2,000; however, he still wanted Harmanson to continue with his search in order to insure that the title to the property was clear.

The total price of the land, including interest, was $5,500. Benjamin then agreed to make two payments of $1,750 within a period of one year, but soon decided that he would like to pay the remaining amount in one payment so he could obtain the deed.

Remember, five years earlier Benjamin had loaned Charles $1,800, which he used to lease the site for his first ship repair facility. No payments had been made on the initial loan. So along with interest that amount had grown to about $2,200. The sum owed on the first loan plus the new loan of $2,000 meant that Charles owed his brother $4,200. Benjamin, after having put his brother in the ship repair business, had continued when possible to support the business venture financially. It now appeared that the ship repair and railway was about to produce a profit and Benjamin was in his right to expect some compensation for all his support.

The conditions set forth by Benjamin after purchasing the property from N. B. Foreman were that if he bought the property the deed would be in his name and he would give Charles a twenty-five-year lease with an interest rate of 6 percent to be paid semiannually. However, Ben further stated that at any time he would extend to Charles the privilege of purchasing half the property at the original price or they could divide the property between them in a manner that would be favorable and fair to both of them.

On November 28, 1880, Benjamin sent Charles $200 to pay for the bond and in January 1881, he sent an additional sum that amounted to somewhere between $500 and $1,000. In March 1882, Benjamin sent $500 to the Honorable W. P. Kellam to charter the "Colonna Dry Dock and Shipbuilding Company." On March 9, 1882, the brothers purchased a small strip of land for forty dollars from the Tucker family heirs. Also in 1882, they bought additional property from E. I. Dupont and the heirs of Thomas A. Hardy.

By 1883, various deeds had passed between the two Colonna brothers and also their neighbors for adjusting land boundaries. On September 15, 1883, Benjamin and Charles, being joint tenants of all the property, decided to settle. During the

Charles J. Colonna, his wife Margaret (above), and his older brother Benjamin (left) were the main people who were involved in the operation of the early shipyard. One could say that they were the "backbone" of the organization.

settlement it was found that Charles owed his brother Benjamin the sum of $5,648.74, which he secured by deed of trust to Benjamin on his undivided half interest.

On Saturday May 24, 1884, all the properties being unencumbered, Charles and Benjamin made a final division. Benjamin having put up most of the money received 46.76 acres. Charles' share amounted to 9.47 acres along the waterfront, which was just what he needed for his shipyard. Since this property included an old colonial farmhouse, Charles was also

This circa 1735 farmhouse was on the first property that Charles and his brother Benjamin purchased in 1880.

afforded a place to live and raise his family. It was on this day that Charles was finally released from all obligations and all accounts between the two brothers were settled.

The property that has been referred to as the Hardy Farm was at the southeast intersection of the Eastern Branch of the Elizabeth River near the Norfolk and Western Railroad tracks. After moving the operation to the newly acquired property Colonna's former location became the site of L. C. Jones' Marine Railway.

On the land purchased from N. D. Foreman stood the previously mention colonial farmhouse. The house, which had been dated to about 1735, faced north and overlooked the Elizabeth River. Benjamin named the house, land, a creek that ran through the property, and a much larger creek nearby, Pescara, for the Adriatic city and river in Italy. In later years the creek that ran through the property was filled and became a part of the shipyard. The larger Creek not only played an important role in the operation of the earlier shipyard, its importance has continued to increase with each year of operation.

The colonial farmhouse became the home of Charles J. Colonna and his wife Margaret. They lived there with their children, most of who had been born in the southwest corner second-story bedroom. In later years, two of their granddaughters, Fannie Mae and Dorothy Evelyn, would also be born in the same room. For twenty-one years the old farmhouse served both as the family residence and the shipyard office. The family lived upstairs and the downstairs served as the office.

Soon after moving into the old colonial farmhouse the size of Charles Colonna's family began to increase and in 1881, Dolly Jones, a young black woman, went to work as a maid for Charles and Margaret Colonna. During the week she lived in the Colonna home and helped with the many family chores. On weekends she went to be with her family who lived in Norfolk off Church Street.

The Death of William A. Graves Sr.

Sometime in the mid-1880s, Charles Colonna's former employer William A. Graves Sr. died, leaving his shipyard to his son William A. Graves Jr. Soon afterwards, Graves Jr. sold the shipyard property in Norfolk to the Old Dominion Steamship Company that ran passenger and freight vessels to New York.

In 1891, William A. Graves Jr. relocated part of his operation to Berkley. On February 20, 1896, Graves bought a parcel of land in Berkley from Benjamin A. Colonna and his wife Fannie B. Colonna and completely relocated his marine business from Water Street in Norfolk to Berkley on the Southside of the Eastern Branch of the Elizabeth River next to Colonna's operation and near the Norfolk and Western Railway. Around 1903 when William A. Graves Jr. went out of business, this property was repurchased by Colonna's and today is the East Yard.

No. 1 Marine Railway

W. A. Graves Sr. originally built the marine railway that became Colonna's No. 1. According to a Norfolk newspaper article dated November 6, 1882, it was in use at Graves Shipyard in Norfolk at that time.

The No. 1 railway was steam driven with a sawmill engine. In 1910 the hauling machine was electrified, and new gears were purchased from Poole Engineering Company of Baltimore, Maryland. The one-hundred-horsepower main electric

The sailing vessel William A. Graves, *built in 1883 by Charles J. Colonna, was eighty-one feet long and carried a crew of six.*

motor would be renewed around 1962. The railway was certified for capacities varying from 500 short tons to 650 short tons with a load concentration capability of 3.7 short tons per foot. Twenty years later, its use was discontinued.

No. 2 Marine Railway

In 1885, a well-to-do shipowner by the name of Culpeper inquired of Charles Colonna why he had not built his railway on piles, and it has been said that Mr. Culpeper proceeded to loan Colonna $7,500 without security to build a new marine railway on a pile foundation. This new railway that became No. 2 was also powered as needed by one or two horses. In 1889, this second marine railway was lengthened and equipped with a steam engine and gear train for hauling. The enlargement was good for a capacity of five hundred tons. The rollers were enlarged to a four-inch diameter by six-inch width, traveling on a flat rail plate, similar to those used in later years. In 1903, the steam engine was replaced by an electric motor. After serving for 122 years it was disassembled in September 2005.

A New County Road

In 1881, when Lycurgus Berkley died, the small community in which he lived in Norfolk County was rated as the most prosperous in the Tidewater region. Around 1883/84 Benjamin Colonna suggested that a direct route was needed in that part of the county between the ferry wharf at the foot of Chestnut Street and the foot of the Campostella Bridge. He laid out a proposed road that would be fifty feet wide and would cross the properties of the Hardy family and that of the Colonna farm.

On February 5, 1885, Charles wrote Benjamin to inform him of a disagreement between the Berkley Ferry Company and the Campostella Bridge Company about the course that the proposed road should take between the Hodges House and the south end of the Campostella Bridge. Benjamin, who at that time, had recently been discharged from the St. Joseph Hospital in Victoria, British Columbia, and was then recuperating aboard the schooner *Yukon*, replied in a letter to Charles, dated February 17, 1885, that he could not attend to the matter firsthand and the main things that he was interested in were that the course of the road cross near where he laid it out and that it was not to be a toll road. If it were to be a toll road, he would be against it crossing through the Colonna farm.

After bickering back and forth among the Ferry Company, the Campostella Bridge Company, the heirs of Thomas A. Hardy and the Colonna brothers, it was decided the road would be a free county road and it would cross the properties of the Colonna brothers, the Hardy heirs, and Main, Liberty, and Virginia Streets to Chestnut Street near the ferry wharf.

Incorporation as a Town

A few years later a group of local politicians began a movement to have that part of Norfolk County incorporated as a town. In a letter dated January 20, 1890, Benjamin A. Colonna wrote in opposition to what was labeled House Bill No. 177, a bill to incorporate that part of Norfolk County into the proposed town of Berkley. Benjamin A. Colonna had several legitimate complaints against the incorporation. To begin with, a few individuals who alone knew its provisions had prepared the charter. He stated that, "the charter was unjust, unwise, and contrary to the well-established principles set forth in the Bill of Rights." He felt that it should be submitted to the people for their consideration and adoption or rejection to be decided by ballot.

The plan was to also include the Colonna Farm into the proposed town of Berkley. Benjamin was outraged because between the two entities there was not a single point of interest. The Colonna post office box was not even in the proposed town. It was located at 999 East Main Street in Norfolk. The Colonna property contained no streets or houses. It was just vacant farmland. As we know, Benjamin had extended to these same people, without charge, the right of way for a new road, fifty feet wide through his land in order to open a direct route between the Ferry Wharf in Berkley and the Campostella Bridge. This road became known as Maple Avenue and today it is Indian River Road. He continued to protest that his land would be taxed and he would receive no benefit from payment of those taxes. Therefore he felt that his farmland should not be included in the proposed town, but should remain a part of Norfolk County.

The town of Berkley was created by an act of the General Assembly of Virginia, which was sponsored by John Middleton Berkley, a resident and a member of the House of Delegates from Norfolk County. The act was approved on March 3, 1890. John M. Berkley, a son of Lycurgus Berkley, was elected the town's first mayor. In the 1890s the town boasted that it was the home of three shipyards and four marine railways.

A document signed by B. A. Colonna, dated July 24, 1890, stated that the property known as *Pescara* "lies just outside the limits of the recently incorporated town of Berkley and partly on each side of the Norfolk and Western Railroad at the south end of their bridge across the Eastern Branch of the Elizabeth River." This statement indicates that Benjamin won his case and the Colonna farm was not included in the town of Berkley.

Early Financial Problems

On at least two different occasions Charles J. Colonna and his wife Margaret had to refinance their part of the property because they were unable to make the payments. By doing this they were able to remain in the shipyard business and also it afforded them a place to live and raise their children.

Steel Floating Dry Docks

In March 1895, Benjamin Azariah Colonna resigned from the Coast and Geodetic Survey and at once began working with his brother Charles at the shipyard. His involvement at the yard led to his study of the latest construction of steel floating dry docks, and to his recommending that their use be adopted in the United States for the purpose of docking large ships such as those used by the Merchant Marines and the US Navy. Senator Chandler, chairman of the US Senate Committee on Naval Affairs, invited him to appear before the committee and Assistant Secretary of the Navy Theodore Roosevelt to give them the benefit of his knowledge on the subject. As a result of his efforts, an appropriation was included in the 1899 federal budget to install the first steel floating dry dock in the United States at a shipyard in New Orleans, Louisiana.

No. 3 Marine Railway

The No. 3 marine railway at Colonna's Shipyard was constructed in 1898 with a steam drive and four-by-six-inch rollers for a capacity of 750 tons. The hauling was done with a one-and-three-quarter-inch stud link chain. However, after several breaks it was determined that the chain was too small. Poole Engineering of Baltimore, Maryland, made a new hauling machine with a two-and-one-eighth-inch iron chain that provided adequate strength against further breaks. In 1915 certain modifications made by James L. Crandall enabled the No. 3 railway to haul as much as 1,500 tons.

Acquisition of Thomas' Boat Yard

In 1899, Charles Colonna purchased the boatyard of one of his competitors, John L. Thomas. Thomas' business, which included two marine railways, was located on the Southern Branch of the Elizabeth River between Water and Montalant Streets in Berkley. Charles later sold the yard to the Norfolk Marine Railway Company, Inc., who in 1933 sold it to the Norfolk Shipbuilding and Dry-Dock Corporation (Norshipco). It has been said that at one time Colonna operated five marine railways.

History of Colonna's Early Properties

It may be of interest to trace the history of the properties that Benjamin A. Colonna and his brother Charles J. Colonna acquired along the Elizabeth River in the vicinity of Berkley in the 1880s. In the late 1880s Benjamin had a careful deed drawn up to cover the properties that throughout the years had so many different owners.

- Beginning in 1813, John Tucker owned the property that became the Colonna Farm.
- E. Barraud and others, commissioners to F. Willson, recorded February 22, 1837.
- F. Willson to W. E. Wood, recorded December 18, 1851.
- W. E. Wood to Eliza J. Willson, recorded January 1, 1856.
- Eliza J. Willson to Robert H. Gordon, recorded April 22, 1856.
- Robert H. Gordon to W. T. Harrison, recorded November 15, 1859.
- W. T. Harrison to John D. Elwell, recorded November 1, 1860.
- John D. Elwell to A. Obendorfer (a street in Berkley was eventually named for Obendorfer), recorded July 17, 1862.
- A. Obendorfer to N. B. Foreman, recorded September 19, 1862.
- N. B. Foreman et ux. [and wife] to Charles J. Colonna, recorded September 29, 1880.

- C. J. Colonna et ux. [and wife] to B. A. Colonna, recorded July 1, 1881.
- The Colonna brothers bought a small strip of property from the Tucker heirs, recorded March 9, 1882.
- B. A. and C. J. Colonna bought property from E. I. Dupont, recorded April 25, 1882.
- B. A. Colonna and C. J. Colonna bought additional property from the Hardy heirs, recorded May 10, 1882.
- B. A. Colonna and C. J. Colonna et ux. [and wife] deed of partition of Pescara, recorded May 24, 1884.
- C. J. Colonna et ux. [and wife] to B. A. Colonna, recorded May 6, 1890.
- B. A. Colonna to C. J. Colonna, recorded May 6, 1890.

When Charles J. Colonna and his wife party of the first part, and Benjamin A. Colonna party of the second part, partitioned the farm between them, the name *Pescara* was given to the tract to distinguish it from other tracts and for easy reference. The name was duly recorded in their deed of partition dated May 24, 1884, and recorded in the clerk's office in the County Court of Norfolk County, Virginia.

The Mystery of John Wilkins Colonna
(1877–1899)

John Wilkins Colonna was the first of seven children to be born to Charles Jones Colonna and his wife Margaret Okeson Dunston. Charles and Margaret were married on Tuesday March 20, 1877, and nine months later on Friday, December 21, John made his appearance into the Colonna family. Eventually, he was joined by one sister and five brothers (one of which died in infancy).

John was the only one of Charles and Margaret's children that was not born in the old colonial farmhouse on shipyard property. In 1877, "Chas. J. Colonna Marine Railway" was still located on property leased from the Hardy family. Most likely he and Margaret were living on Brewer Street in Norfolk, Virginia, when their first child was born.

It was in late 1880 when the family moved into the colonial farmhouse on shipyard property. So John Wilkins did spend most of his short life living in the old house. After reaching adulthood he went to work at the Azariah Jones Shipyard in Brooklyn, New York, which was owned by his maternal grandfather.

The Jones Shipyard was noted for building exceptionally fast square-rigger sailing ships that were used in the California Gold Rush and in the China/London tea trade. Once a year sailing vessels loaded with tea departed China and made a mad dash for London. The first ships to arrive usually got the best price for their cargo.

John's sister Margaret Evelyn Colonna and Henry Francis McCoy had made plans to be married at the farmhouse on shipyard property (*Pescara*) on Wednesday, September 20, 1899. Being a loving brother, naturally John wanted to attend the grand affair so he left New York a few days before in order to arrive home in time for the wedding. When John didn't show up on the appointed day, the young couple went ahead with the ceremony that would make them man and wife.

So why didn't John make it home in time for the wedding? After all he left Brooklyn in plenty of time. Here is the beginning of a mystery that would have no closure for almost fifty years. Much of the following story is based on assumptions or speculations.

When John's whereabouts could not be determined, his father Charles J. Colonna and others made every effort and spared no expense in trying to locate him. Weeks, months, and years passed and not a single trace could be uncovered. It was as if he had just vanished in thin air. Of course there were supposedly many sightings at various locations and times. These people were certain that they knew exactly where he was and for a substantial amount of cash they would relinquish that information to the family.

After a while Charles J. and other members of the family gave up all hope of ever learning where he might be or what may have happened to him. Forty-nine years would pass and only his brothers and sister were still alive and interested in why he had not been found. It was a Sunday morning in 1948 that Ben Colonna Sr., one of John's brothers, received a rather strange phone call from a man who wanted to meet him on the old Norfolk airport road. The man told Ben that he had information about his missing brother. Being uncertain and probably a little afraid of meeting a strange man on a rather deserted road, Ben Sr. called his son Ben Jr. and asked if he had a gun. He told him the story about the phone call and asked if he would follow him to the airport road, bring his gun, and stay about one hundred feet behind his car.

With all the details worked out, father and son headed to the airport road. As they arrived and parked their cars, an old man not too well dressed, and walking with a cane, approached Ben Sr. They walked side by side and talked for about half an hour. Ben Jr., with a sharp eye on what was taking place and his hand on the pistol in his pocket, stood some distance away from the two men. Ben Sr. then walked away from the man and told his son to leave and meet him at the shipyard.

Upon meeting at the shipyard Ben Sr. told his son the following story that had been relayed to him by the stranger on the airport road. The man was a retired engineer for the Norfolk and Southern Railroad and a friend of a Mr. Keeter, who was also a retired railroad engineer. Mr. Keeter had given him a detailed explanation of what had happened to John Wilkins Colonna in Edenton, North Carolina, many years before (1899). Mr. Keeter was a very old man and wanted the truth known before he passed away. However, he did not want to tell the story himself because he feared that he might lose his railroad retirement. It seems that Keeter knew what happened and had kept the details to his self for almost fifty years.

John had arrived in Norfolk a few days before the wedding of his sister. Knowing the engineer who was possibly Mr. Keeter, he was able to hitch a ride on a Norfolk and Southern train to Edenton, North Carolina, where he planned to visit a girl friend and then return to Norfolk the next day. It seems that he had done this several times in the past. Of course it was against railroad rules for him to ride in the engine with the engineer; however, he was told that he could ride in the empty refrigerator car where he would be out of sight. John agreed and the engineer said he would blow the train whistle at the switch in Edenton and John could get off.

As planned, the engineer blew the whistle and assumed that John had gotten out of the refrigerator car and headed into town. But while shifting the railroad cars on the tracks a body that had been run over by the train, was discovered. There were four men working with the train and the one who discovered the body called all of them together. It was dark so each man brought his lantern. When looking at the body they were all in total shock for they recognized it as being that of John Colonna, which each man knew and had seen many times in the past.

The thought was that after hearing the whistle John awoke and being half asleep climbed out of the ice loading hole in the top of the refrigerator car and while climbing down the ladder attached to the car to reach the ground he fell on the tracks and was run over by a shifting railroad car.

The four men were terrified and did not know what to do. They all knew that what had taken place was against railroad policy. They also realized that they all could possibly go to jail if the law found out about it and if railroad supervision found out they would definitely lose their jobs. So they all decided to place him in a wooden packing or toolbox and bury him alongside the tracks in Edenton, North Carolina.

After having received this information and believing it to be true, Ben Sr. and his brother Will, younger brothers of John, contacted the Norfolk and Southern Railroad about digging alongside the railroad tracks in Edenton, North Carolina. They were told if they would sign legal papers agreeing not to sue the railroad that permission would be granted. The brothers agreed not to sue and the dig was approved. Ben and Will decided if any of the remains were recovered that they would have them buried in Elmwood Cemetery in Norfolk alongside his father and mother Charles J. and Margaret Colonna.

John Wilkins Colonna (1877–1899) was the first of seven children born to Charles J. Colonna and his wife Margaret. He disappeared in 1899. Forty-nine years passed before the mystery of his disappearance was solved.

Of the original crew of four railroad employees that had buried John in 1899, two were still living and one of them was very elderly and very sick. As a matter of fact after providing information as to the burial site, two days later he died. The local sheriff was contacted and with his assistance and information received from the remaining railroad crewman, a large-scale dig was begun. A trench about five feet wide, three to four feet deep, and about a city block long was dug and the dirt was carefully shifted. A few bones were found and taken to a local doctor who could not determine if they were the bones of a human or a small animal.

The consensus was that the burial site identified by the two members of the crew that had been present in 1899 was correct; however, the exact site had most likely been disturbed earlier by the widening of the nearby highway.

With the endless effort made by his father Charles J. Colonna, the new information provided, and the extensive dig made in Edenton, North Carolina, by John's brothers Ben and Will, this terrible family tragedy was finally put to rest with the confidence that all that could be done had been done and at last the mystery of John Wilkins Colonna's disappearance was known.

Marriage Ceremonies at *Pescara*

Throughout the years many special events took place at the old farmhouse, which earlier had been given the name *Pescara*. One such event was the marriage of Charles' second child, and only daughter, Margaret Evelyn to Henry Francis McCoy in September 1899. Margaret had been born in 1880. Before ending in divorce her marriage to Henry produced two children, Margaret Colonna and Clara Evelyn.

On January 14, 1925, Clara Evelyn McCoy married Waverly Lee Berkley Jr. thus forming a connection between the Colonna and Berkley families.

The death of Henry Francis McCoy occurred under rather unusual circumstances. His brother Russell received two letters. The first letter, dated February 21, 1915, stated that Henry had been found unconscious on a railroad station platform in Fairbank, Arizona, and taken by train to the hospital at Douglas, Arizona, which was the nearest place where medical assistance was available.

The second letter dated February 24, 1915, stated that Henry had died. According to the autopsy report his death was due to cerebral concussion. Since there were no fractures or evidence of violence it was determined that he must have fallen from a railroad train. The station agent in Fairbank found the barely alive body on the station platform where it had been placed and covered with a blanket.

In 1920, Margaret Evelyn remarried. Her second husband was Oscar Francis Smith Jr., founder of Norfolk Dredging Company. This marriage also ended in divorce, after which Margaret Evelyn Colonna McCoy Smith spent the rest of her ninety-seven years living by herself in her home in the Oaklette section of what is now the Washington Borough of the city of Chesapeake, Virginia.

Carl Dunston Colonna Sr.

Carl Dunston Colonna Sr. was born May 31, 1881, in the old colonial farmhouse on shipyard property in Norfolk County, Virginia. He was the first of four Colonna brothers to attend the private school that was operated by the Reverend Robert Gatewood who had served as a chaplain in the War Between the States. He opened his school located beside his home as soon as the "Yankees" cleared the area. Later, Carl attended Norfolk Academy.

In the spring of 1903, Carl and the rest of the family were making final preparations and sprucing up the old farmhouse for his upcoming marriage to Pearl Sykes on March 18, 1903. Pearl had been born at Mount Pleasant, Norfolk County. It has been said that her father George was a gallant soldier of the Confederacy in the War Between the States.

Needless to say, Carl wanted everything to be

Carl Dunston Colonna Sr. was born May 31, 1881, in the old farmhouse on shipyard property. On March 18, 1903, Carl married Pearl Sykes in the same house.

just right for the occasion so he spent a considerable amount of time and effort in polishing his buggy and making certain that his favorite white horse was perfectly clean and standing tall. All was well until after the ceremony when someone went to the barn to get the horse. Lo and behold the horse had been painted to look like a zebra. Carl was furious! Of course he never found out who did such an awful thing to his beautiful white horse. He always suspected his brothers but was never able to prove it. Who else would have done such an awful thing?

As the story goes, a substitute horse was located but it was nothing like Carl's white horse. However, it was good enough to pull the highly polished buggy; and both Carl and Pearl were happy to be married and were looking forward to all the pleasures that would accompany a delightful honeymoon.

Carl was a very active member of St. Paul's Protestant Episcopal Church in Norfolk and later became a member of the St. Brides Church in Berkley where he sang in the choir and taught Sunday school. He was also interested in civic affairs, and became a member of the Norfolk chamber of Commerce, and the Hampton Roads Maritime Exchange.

Other Happenings at *Pescara*

There were more than a few strange occurrences at the old farmhouse. The Colonna children enjoyed roasting nuts that came from the hickory tree just outside the front door. There always seemed to be a race to see who could gather the most nuts. One morning young Ben awoke first and quietly sneaked down the stairs, only to be frightened by a lady with long black hair and clothed in a full-length white dress sitting on the sofa in their living room. He ran back upstairs and told his father who immediately went downstairs to find no one on the sofa as well as anywhere else in the house. Charles said that his young son Benjamin had described his deceased mother in great detail including the specific dress in which she was buried. Benjamin was too young to have remembered anything about his mother's funeral or the dress she wore. It seemed that she had made a special visit to see how the family was managing without her assistance. Benjamin lived to be eighty-five years old. Until the day he died, the image of that beautiful lady some eighty years earlier was so strong that there was no doubt in his mind that he had seen his mother that morning. Benjamin's mother, Margaret Okeson Dunston Colonna, had died of pneumonia on July 15, 1892.

This circa 1735 farmhouse was on the first property that Charles and his brother Benjamin purchased in 1880. Charles and his family lived upstairs and the shipyard office was on the first floor.

On Christmas Eve, it was a family custom for the children to take turns talking up the chimney to Santa Clause and telling him what they wanted for Christmas. On one particular Christmas Eve it was young Benjamin's turn and after having completed his wishes to Santa, he proceeded to move from the chimney and in the process bumped his head very hard. He then yelled up the chimney, "Damn you Santa Clause!" His father Charles, being a strict disciplinarian, immediately administered a licking to that part of the anatomy where he figured it would do the most good.

Chapter II

1900–1925

In the spring of 1900, after a separation of about five years from his family, Benjamin Azariah Colonna decided to sell his local interest and return to his home in Washington, D.C. By that time the land that had been referred to as the Colonna farm had been amicably divided into parcels between the two brothers. By the end of the year Charles J. Colonna was operating two marine railways on the Eastern Branch of the Elizabeth River with capacities of four hundred tons and fifteen hundred tons.

Benjamin Sells His Parcels and Retires

Benjamin sold his parcels three times. The first two buyers could not make their payments and therefore forfeited their equity. The third buyer, Norfolk and Western Railway, purchased the property in order to expand their coal pier operation. This third buyer was able to make the necessary payments and clear its note. The end result was that Benjamin received $65,000, a much larger sum from the sale of his part of the farm than he ever expected. The money acquired was put to good use, for he invested it in his family home in Washington, D.C. Even after his retirement Benjamin continued to make monthly trips to Norfolk in order to visit his brother Charles, to attend to the financial end of the shipyard business, and to help Charles in other ways as needed.

Charles J. Remarries and Relocates

On January 30, 1902, Charles Jones Colonna at the age of fifty-two married his second wife, twenty-three-year-old Fannie Cornick Fentress. Charles and Fannie would have one child, a son, Bruce Cornick Colonna, who was born in 1903. The new Mrs. Colonna did not like living in the old farmhouse and being in the midst of a shipyard that was bustling with activity; so soon after the wedding Charles purchased a three-story house at 801 Colonial Avenue in Norfolk,

Benjamin O. Colonna Sr. and three of his brothers received their early education at the school run by The Reverend Robert Gatewood, who stands at left. Charles Jones Colonna, founder of Colonna's Shipyard, is seated at right in the swing. Charles' second wife Fannie Cornick Fentress Colonna is holding their infant son Bruce Cornick Colonna, born in 1903. Dolly Jones, the maid, stands in back. Benjamin O. Colonna Sr. is seated in front and his brother Edward Holt Colonna stands at right.

Virginia. The house, which was built in 1889, still stands (2011) on the northwest corner of Redgate and Colonial Avenues.

After moving to the Colonial Avenue residence Charles and Fannie hired a new maid. Dolly Jones, who had served the family well for several years, was from the old school; she had no formal training and also did not like the idea of wearing the required maid's uniform. The thought was that Dolly just would not fit into the social climate expected at the new address.

So as a result of this change in address, what happened to Dolly Jones? Dolly was hired by Benjamin O. Colonna Sr. and worked for his family until 1938, thus completing fifty-seven years of faithful service to the Colonna family.

Soon after Charles and Fannie moved, the entire farmhouse became the business office for the shipyard. In 1927 the old house was still standing, but is thought to have been demolished two years later. The original kitchen off the back served as a lunchroom for shipyard workers and its usefulness outlasted that of the main structure.

The wooden sailing vessel Barque Belstone *was built in Quebec, Canada, in 1872. It is shown here on marine railway number 3 at Colonna Dry Dock and Shipbuilding Company in 1902.*

Hard Times

In the process of enlarging the shipyard operation and moving to Colonial Avenue, Colonna may have over extended himself and the business once again fell on hard times. It has been said that his wife Fannie took in sewing and sold off most of her inherited family furniture in order to help keep the business operational. As a result of perseverance and constant and careful oversight the shipyard was once

In the early 1900s, Charles J. Colonna purchased this three-story house at 801 Colonial Avenue in Norfolk, Virginia. In 1920, he died in the second-story bedroom that was located in the turret facing Colonial Avenue. The house still stands in the year 2011.

again saved. Business began to increase, and six years later the railway capacity was again increased, this time to two thousand tons.

Fox and Gordon

As previously stated, in 1903 William A. Graves Jr., not really liking the shipyard business, sold the Graves Shipyard and Marine Railway in Berkley to the Colonna Marine Railway firm. The Graves operation was located on the Southside of the Eastern Branch of the Elizabeth River east of the Norfolk and Western Railway. After this Colonna supervised all the regular repairs at the shipyard except the steel, boiler, and machine work. He contracted those jobs to the company of Fox and Gordon who operated out of a brick building and office on the property. After selling his business, Graves Jr. went to work for Merritt and Chapman Derrick and Wrecking Company. In 1904, his son Robert became an assistant foreman at Colonna's Marine Railway.

Unusual Conversion and Construction of F/V

In 1904, Charles J. Colonna, president and founder of Colonna Marine Railway, contacted master ship carpenter William S. Brustar of Pocomac City, Maryland, to build a tugboat for a customer. When the tug was near completion, the customer went broke; but, as luck would have it about that time the Seaboard Oil and Guano Company of Reedville, Virginia, asked Colonna if he could build a menhaden fishing boat for them. Giving the request some thought, Charles came up with the idea of cutting the near completed tug in half and adding a new and larger midsection. But before attempting a task such as that he felt it would be best to build a model made of wood to determine if it would be practical and to check the appearance of the newly shaped hull. This was done and the conversion was approved. Mr. Brustar stayed on and supervised this unusual conversion and construction. The boat was built of wood and was powered by a 450-horsepower steam engine. Once completed, the boat remained active as a menhaden fishing boat for many years. It operated mostly in the Chesapeake Bay area. The vessel was later renamed *A. Vernon McNeal*. The wooden model that played such an important part in the project is owned by Colonna's Shipyard and now hangs near the boardroom on the third floor of the main office building.

Colonna Marine Railways, Inc.

The town of Berkley was short-lived. By order of the Circuit Court of Norfolk County, Berkley became the Eighth Ward of the city of Norfolk. On January 1, 1906, Berkley was officially annexed by Norfolk. Shortly after the annexation Colonna was operating five marine railways and repairing an average of 650 vessels each year.

On March 30, 1907, Judge William Nathaniel Portlock of the Circuit Court of Norfolk County signed the certificate of incorporation of the Colonna Marine Railway. It was then that Charles J. Colonna largely abated his individual activities in connection with the shipyard business that he had founded and developed. His original plan was to sell the business, but his sons pleaded with him to give them the opportunity to run the operation. Will, hoping to help persuade his father not to sell the yard, left the Virginia Polytechnic Institute (VPI) where he had been studying mechanical engineering for two years and went to work at the ship-

This photograph of the F/V (fishing vessel) Charles J. Colonna *was taken in January 1956. The original vessel, which was built in 1904, was made of wood and was powered by steam. Coal was used for fuel. Sometimes, in order to increase its capacity, a wooden vessel was cut and a section was added near its center.*

A note on the back of this photo said: "To W. W. Colonna from Chesapeake Corporation in appreciation of service performed in conversion of Diesel Tug Wm. P. Congdon *completed May 1938." The tug was renamed* Chesapeake.

yard. After giving it some thought Charles decided to put his sons to a practical test and if they were successful as he had been, he would sell the business to them.

The officers and directors at that time became: Willoughby W. Colonna, president and general manager; Benjamin O. Colonna, vice president; and Carl D. Colonna, secretary and treasurer. The three officers along with Charles J. Colonna and Isaac O. Diggs constituted the Board of Directors. By being a member of the Board of Directors, Charles could oversee their activities firsthand. So his sons Willoughby Warren, Benjamin Okeson, and Carl Dunston were put to the test and over a period of five years they met with their father's approval. With the knowledge that his sons would continue to run the business as he had with honesty, fairness, customer satisfaction, and also at a profit, Charles J. Colonna retired entirely from its management in 1912. By all indications, Charles held their note for at least $90,000.

A Presidential Ride—William Howard Taft

By 1909, Charles J. Colonna was the proud owner of the second automobile in Norfolk. It is not certain what the make was, but A. Wrenn and Sons of Nor-

Colonna Marine Railway circa 1910.

In 1909, Charles J. Colonna was the proud owner of the second automobile in Norfolk, Virginia. This photograph was taken at his home on Colonial Avenue.

folk, Maker of Carriages and Wagons built a few early automobiles. However, the automobile in the surviving photograph resembles one of the Ramblers that were in production at that time.

Of special interest was the visit to Norfolk of William Howard Taft, the newly elected twenty-seventh president of the United States and later the tenth chief justice of the US Supreme Court. A party and reception had been arranged for Taft at the Casino. The president's rail car arrived at Cape Henry and waiting for him in front of the train station was an automobile, which was a real curiosity at that time. This horseless carriage was the property of Captain Charles Colonna, proprietor of Colonna Marine Railways. The automobile had been shipped ahead to Cape Henry on a flatbed railway car. President Taft climbed into Colonna's automobile and they rode in a straight line down the brick walk from the station to O'Keefe's Restaurant, a distance of about one hundred yards. Everyone who could possibly be there showed up. Information originating from a Doctor Woodhouse stated that O'Keefe was planning a beauty contest for that special day. The contestants were to be oysters, large flavorful oysters. He offered a prize for the prettiest barrel of oysters brought in by his regular suppliers. It has been said that

Taft, who was known as the large man who was president from 1909 to 1913 had an enormous appetite, especially for oysters. President Taft was over six feet tall and weighed 332 pounds at the time of his inauguration.

Vanderbilt Yacht

On the morning of April 14, 1914, the yacht *Tarantula*, owned by William K. Vanderbilt arrived from Florida for overhaul at Colonna's Marine Railway. The vessel, which was described as a veritable floating palace, cost $140,000 to build. E. H. Harding, captain of the *Tarantula* and his wife visited with Mrs. H. L. West at 18 Hardy Avenue in Berkley while the vessel was undergoing repairs. When repairs were completed, Vanderbilt came from New York and rode the yacht back home.

George Lawley and Son Corporation in 1912 had built the *Tarantula* at Neponset, Massachusetts. The vessel was acquired from William K. Vanderbilt by the US Navy on April 25, 1917, was converted to a patrol boat, and operated along the coastal waters of Connecticut, New York, and New Jersey until October 28, 1918, when she sank after colliding with the Royal Holland Lloyd Line SS *Frisia*. Vanderbilt was subsequently paid $75,000 to cover its value.

Marine Iron Works Company, Inc.

On December 5, 1917, B. O. Colonna, W. W. Colonna, and W. B. Drury established Marine Iron Works Company, Inc. The business encompassed general marine supply and repair work, was engaged in the general machine shop business and did general repairing and construction work, it bought and sold, repaired, supplied and installed machinery, tools, boilers, shafting and other appliances, and carried on a general marine supply and repair works. The certificate of incorporation was granted by the State Corporation Commission on December 27, 1917, and was filed with the Secretary of the Commonwealth for recordation on the same date.

Norfolk Lighterage Company

December 12, 1917, the Norfolk Lighterage Company, Inc., was established. The officers and Board of Directors were B. O Colonna, president; J. B. Ransone, vice president; and W. W. Colonna, secretary and treasurer.

The S/S Powhatan *shown here on number 3 railway at Colonna Marine Railway circa 1917 was built in Chester, Pennsylvania, in 1894.*

The purpose of the corporation was to engage in owning and operating vessels for the purpose of lightering, wrecking and dredging; to engage in general stevedoring business; to load and unload vessels of every description; to handle freight, cargo, or ballast wherever stored, and to do general hauling; to own, lease, charter and operate dredges, barges, tugs, launches, scows, and all other floating equipment necessary to the performance of such work.

In the 1920s and early to mid-1930s the company owned and operated about ten steam tugboats and thirty wooden barges. The fleet worked mostly in and around the port of Hampton Roads, Virginia. However, at times it worked in the Chesapeake Bay and James River also in Virginia as well as the canals, rivers, and sounds of North Carolina. On occasion one of the tugs would tow barges carrying paper pulp and sugar from Philadelphia, Pennsylvania, to Savannah, Georgia. By unanimous consent, on November 2, 1936, the company was dissolved. The Certificate of Dissolution was dated November 7, 1936.

World War I Years

During World War I the shipyard thrived. It was engaged in repairing Fifth Naval District vessels that guarded the capes. Repairs were also accomplished on warships, Army transports, and vessels that were operated by the US Shipping

Board, as well as commercial ships when possible. After World War I, business continued to flourish and in early 1919, the officers began to consider filing papers with the State Corporation Commission to amend the charter; however, no action would be taken until 1921.

First Major Shipyard Threat

Throughout the history of the shipyard there were several threats of such magnitude that they actually endangered the survival of the business. Of course occasionally a problem would surface where somebody would fail to pay for work completed and while those problems certainly affected the bottom line profit for the year they did not pose a severe threat to the overall existence of the operation. There may have been some in Charles J. Colonna's day, but none presented the risk that took place near the end of and immediately following World War I and a second threat in later years that would lead the shipyard into bankruptcy.

The first real threat took place near the end of World War I when the US Navy Department approached Captains Will and Ben Colonna and asked them to attend a meeting in Washington, D.C., to discuss construction of a huge marine railway. Word from the Navy Department was that they desperately needed another large lift to accommodate Navy work and to increase competition in the port of Hampton Roads. The Colonna brothers wanted to know if there would be enough Navy work after the war to offset the cost of building such a marine railway. The Navy representatives assured them that there would be.

A meeting of the Board of Directors of the Colonna Marine Railway Corporation was held at their office in Norfolk, Virginia, on June 5, 1918, to discuss the need for and the advantages to be gained in building such a large marine railway. It was agreed to seek bids for its construction and later the Board agreed to accept the bid of $232,000 received from Crandall Engineers, Inc., of Massachusetts to build a new forty-five-hundred-ton six-chain marine railway. Work was begun in 1919 and it was completed in 1920. Paul Crandall who designed the railway said it was the largest wooden marine railway in the world.

However, after the war the League of Nations was formed with US President Woodrow Wilson as its chairman. As a result of this action the US Navy was greatly downsized and the promised Navy contracts did not materialize. Without this anticipated work and the debt incurred by building the larger railway, the yard fell on hard times. This would be one of several times throughout its

On May 20, 1921, both the Rescue *and the* Merritt Chapman and Scott *tugs were dry-docked on Colonna's Marine Railway in Norfolk, Virginia.*

history that the shipyard would find itself in a position such as this. It was a real struggle to make payments on the loan of $232,000 and on several occasions the shipyard was almost forced to close.

No. 4—Crandall Railway

The new railway became known as No. 4 and was later referred to as the Crandall Railway. It would be Colonna's largest ship lift until the eighteen-thousand-ton floating dry dock was purchased in 1986. No. 4 railway was completely rebuilt in 1965 and new chain and chain wheels were installed in 1981. On March 10, 1982, it was examined and found to be safe and adequate to dock vessels up to four thousand short tons. At the time of this writing the Crandall marine railway has served the shipyard faithfully for about ninety years.

Soon after completion in 1920, the USS *Mars* became the first big ship to be dry-docked on No. 4. It has been said that many people came from miles around to witness this event. There was some doubt as to whether the railway could lift this large ship out of the water. The doubt was so great that those present were actually making bets among themselves as to what the final outcome would be.

Construction of the Inside Machine Shop

In 1920 the original inside machine shop was built near where the present-day main entrance gate is located. The concrete used in its construction was mixed in wheelbarrows and transported by way of ramps, to where it was needed. The original machines used in the shop were made of cast iron and were belt driven. There was one manually operated 3.5-ton overhead crane that was used to service the shop. When completed this machine shop was considered to be one of the largest and best on the East Coast. The old weld lathe, which dates back to the late nineteenth century, is still in use. Since the creation of Steel America the operation has more than doubled in size and capabilities. The majority of its work now (2011) comes from customers other than the shipyard.

Marine Iron Works/Colonna
Marine Railway—Merger

Meetings of the stockholders and the Board of Directors were held in the office of Colonna Marine Railway on December 5, 1921. W. W. Colonna, B. O. Colonna, and W. B. Drury were all of the stockholders as well as officers of the Board of Directors. The question of merger of Marine Iron Works with Colonna Marine Railway was discussed. It was deemed advisable and in the best interest of the two corporations that Marine Iron Works and Colonna Marine Railway merge and form one corporation. Motions were made, duly seconded, and unanimously resolved that the two entities would merge and become known as Colonna's Shipyard, Inc.

The Certificate of Merger was signed by the Secretary of the Commonwealth—Department of the State Corporation Commission on December 31,

The USS Mars was the first ship dry-docked on number 4 marine railway. The ship was so big that people came from miles around to see if it could be pulled out of the water and on the new marine railway, circa 1921.

1921, and by the Clerk of the Norfolk County Circuit Court on January 9, 1922. The Commonwealth of Virginia, Department of the State Corporation Commission received $5.00 on December 31, 1921. One dollar was for tax on the seal, one dollar was for the clerk's fee, and three dollars for entering, issuing, and certifying the merger. Because of the merger five thousand shares of common stock were reissued.

The officers and directors of the merged company for the first year were W. W. Colonna, president; B. O. Colonna, vice president; W. B. Drury, second vice president; and Carl D. Colonna, secretary and treasurer.

December 29, 1922, the officers of the shipyard were W. W. Colonna, president; B. O. Colonna, vice president; C. D. Colonna, secretary and treasurer; W. B. Drury, second vice president; S. D. Barnes, superintendent of wood repairs; and R. B. Duncan, assistant secretary. At that time there were four marine railways: No. 1—500 tons; No. 2—750 tons; No. 3—1,500 tons; and No. 4 (also referred to as the Crandall marine railway)—4,500 tons.

Norwegian Tramp Steamer *Arna*

In 1922, Colonna's Shipyard was awarded a contract to scrape and paint the bottom of the Norwegian tramp steamer *Arna*. At that time it was the largest ship ever to be hauled out on a marine railway in Norfolk. The *Arna* was a vessel of 5,264 gross tons and was 410 feet in length. Even though she was a big ship, the railway was capable of handling a ship even forty feet longer.

Prior to the installation of the Crandall railway in 1920, the largest vessel ever hauled out at the Norfolk yard was said to be the steamer *Pennsylvania*, which was used as a ferry between Norfolk and Cape Charles.

Rumrunners

The Eighteenth Amendment—which prohibited the manufacture, transportation, and sale of alcoholic liquor for use as beverages—was proclaimed in effect on January 16, 1920, one year after ratification. It remained in effect for nearly fourteen years, until it was repealed in December 1933.

There is always that certain group of people that will try to circumvent the law. In this case the groups operated aboard ships and engaged in smuggling liquor. Those folks became known as rumrunners. It then became the job of the US Coast Guard to enforce that part of the national prohibition law. In order to do this they needed a fleet of faster boats. That's where Colonna's Shipyard, Inc., entered the picture.

In early 1924, they were awarded a quarter-million-dollar contract to build ten speedboats to be used by the Coast Guard in its work of enforcing the national prohibition laws. The boats, which were built simultaneously, were each seventy-two feet in length, and were equipped with two two-hundred-horsepower Sterling engines with twin screws that would develop a speed of eighteen knots. The Coast Guard provided the engines and guns. By August 1924, construction of the boats was about 15 percent complete.

The first of the boats, *CG-223*, was launched before a large crowd of spectators at 1:20 on Monday afternoon, October 6, 1924. She was decorated with flags and bunting and when striking the waters of the Elizabeth River, it glided safely and gracefully, indicating that her construction was flawless.

Glenn Perry Colonna, who was nine years old, christened the boat by breaking a bottle across its bow. This was the first launching of a government boat at

Norfolk in several years. Each of the remaining nine boats took to the water at intervals of about thirty days. Construction of the ten boats under contract was completed in June 1925.

Among the invited guests at the launching were City Manager Causey and Mayor Tyler of Norfolk; Rear Admiral H. G. Ziegemeier, commandant of the Norfolk Navy Yard; and Chief of Police Ironmonger and City Sergeant Tumbleson also of Norfolk. CG-223 was completed (guns, etc., were installed) and turned over to the US Coast Guard on October 16, 1924.

One of the more interesting stages of the construction process was that in which a steam box was used to mold the solid ribs that were made of Virginia and North Carolina white oak. Ninety men were employed in construction of the Coast Guard vessels. These were in addition to the more than 150 already engaged in repairs and other work at the shipyard.

Periodic inspections made by construction officers of the Coast Guard revealed that the progress made at the Colonna's Shipyard was much greater than that of all the other shipyards involved in building the new speedboats. Before the program was completed, shipyards on both the East and West Coasts built three hundred of the boats. Colonna's original bid was for construction of fifty of them.

Disaster on Railway No. 4

In March 1925, disaster struck on No. 4 railway when three seamen were engaged in cleaning and painting the inside of a lifeboat. The trip release was accidentally struck by one of the floorboards causing one end of the boat to drop. All three men were spilled from the boat and dropped about forty feet to the bottom of the railway. The men all received broken necks and died almost instantly. It was said that one man tried to jump into the water beyond the railway uprights, but failed. The accident resulted into a long and in-depth case in Admiralty Law.

Wooden Cargo Ship

In the 1920s a wooden cargo ship, whose name has since slipped into the past, pulled into Colonna's Shipyard for repairs. The ship had been built on the West Coast of the United States around the time of the First World War. Lumber was plentiful at that time and a considerable amount had been used

The remains of the old wooden ship, known as the "Gas-Free-Boat," can still be seen near Pier No. 1 in the East Yard. The vessel burned to the water line in the 1920s.

in construction of this well-built vessel. The ship was equipped with a steam engine for power and with cargo booms both fore and aft of the pilothouse.

The owner wanted to use an acetylene torch to do some burning in the engine room and Captain Ben Colonna said, "absolutely not," that there was "too much oil in the bilges" and the "risk of fire" was too great. The owner then asked for permission to hire a burner himself and do the job in the shipyard. Again the answer was no. The owner then made arrangements to take the ship next door to the Atlantic Creosote Plant dock where he hired a burner to do the job. It wasn't long before a fire broke out and the vessel burned to the waterline.

The old hull was about fifty-three inches thick in places and was very well put together. On one occasion a floating derrick with a clamshell bucket was used in an attempt to tear the hull apart in order to remove it. But being unsuc-

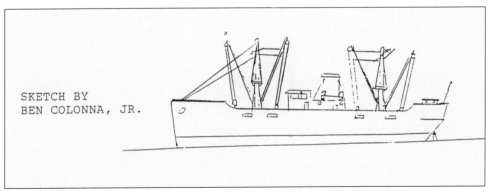

Sketch of the wooden cargo ship by Ben Colonna Jr.

The launching of CG-228, one of ten US Coast Guard speedboats built by Colonna's Shipyard, took place in late 1924.

cessful and afraid of damaging his rig in the process, the owner gave up. The remains of the old wooden ship were left just east of the Norfolk and Western Railway on Colonna's Shipyard property that had once been a part of the Graves Shipyard.

Throughout the years several young boys while swimming would dive into the cargo hole, which was under water, come up under the submerged decks, become disoriented and not being able to find the way out, they would drown.

It has been said that the outline of the ship's remains were included in an old shipyard land plot and Captain Will Colonna wrote the name of the ship next to its outline. At this time the old shipyard land plot has not been found and possibly does not still exist.

Chapter III

1925–1955

Four-Masted Schooner—*Constellation*

In 1935, the owners of Colonna's Shipyard advertised that they were ship builders and made repairs to both steel and wooden vessels. In July of that year the four-masted schooner *Constellation* was on number four railway at Colonna's. It had been brought into the yard for rudder repairs, cleaning and painting of its bottom, cutting out and renewing damaged parts of the keel, and possibly other repairs. The repairs required the work of carpenters, caulkers, machinist, boiler-makers and several trade helpers. The full charges for all the work accomplished came to the large sum of $690.59.

The arrival of this four-masted schooner at Colonna's Shipyard in 1935 was indicative of the late day of sailing vessels.

This five-masted schooner was the last of its kind to dock at Colonna's Shipyard in 1937.

The Menhaden Fish Factory

An industry that thrived during the first half of the twentieth century on the East Coast of the United States was the fishing industry. It had a significant effect on the lives of the people living near the Chesapeake Bay in general and the Rappahannock River in particular. There were many fishing vessels that at the end of each day brought their catch and unloaded it at what became known as fish factories. One such facility was the Menhaden Fish Factory at Taft Beach near Whitestone, Virginia. The menhaden is a herring-like West Atlantic fish that is important as a source of oil and fertilizer.

After a series of operations the fish were dumped on a conveyor that transported them to a cooker. The cooker consisted of a screw conveyor housed in a steel pipe about fifteen or sixteen inches in diameter. Steam was then injected into the pipe at approximately every twelve inches for a distance of about thirty feet. As the screw moved the raw fish through the pipe, the steam cooked them. After emerging from the cooker the fish went through a press that pressed the oil and water from the fish solids. These solid particles were made up of the bones and flesh of the cooked fish. The particles were then dried and bagged. The end result was fishmeal that was shipped to fertilizer plants. The oil and water pressed from the fish were separated and the fish oil was used mostly in manufacturing paint.

This painting by Casey Holtzinger shows the Menhaden Fish Factory at Taft Beach in Whitestone, Virginia, as it appeared in 1932.

It was in the year 1912, that H. R. Humphreys Sr. built a factory for Dr. B. H. B. Hubbard Jr. and Wilbur James who then gave it the name Taft Fish Company. Little is known about this factory until B. O. Colonna Sr. and his brother W. W. Colonna Sr. bought it in 1933. The Colonna brothers owned the motor vessel *Virginia Dare*, which was used to haul the factory's output of fish scrap to market in Norfolk. After which the vessel went to Lambert's Point coal pier, took on a load of coal, and carried it back to the factory where it would be used by the fishing vessels. The brothers operated the factory under the name Menhaden Products, Inc., until 1939 when they sold it to J. Howard Smith Sr., of Port Monmouth, New Jersey. This was a side business for the brothers who were owners of Colonna's Shipyard in the Berkley section of Norfolk.

Atlantic Fishing Company and Menhaden Fishing Vessels—1950s

The fishing vessels (F/V) *Charles J. Colonna*, *W. W. Colonna*, and *B. O. Colonna* were designed, owned, and outfitted by the brothers Captains Ben and Will Colonna who operated them as the Atlantic Fishing Company and used them in catching millions of menhaden fish from the waters of the Atlantic Coast from New York to Morehead City, North Carolina. These steel-hulled diesel engine powered vessels were outfitted with the most modern fishing equipment of the time. Schools of fish were spotted by an observer from the crow's nest and were also spotted by airplanes with radio contact.

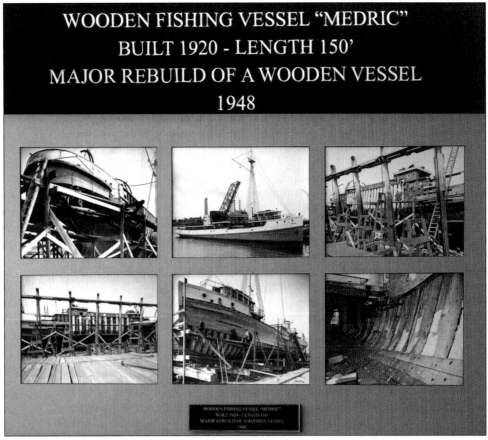

This series of photographs displays a major rebuilding of the wooden fishing vessel Medric *in 1948. The boat, which was 150 feet in length, was built in 1920.*

Once the fish were captured in the nets they were processed and the meal that was produced was used primarily for cattle and poultry feed in the United States and was made into flour for human consumption in European countries. The fish oil that was produced was used for paint and linoleum in the United States and margarine in Europe. Each year these boats began fishing the Chesapeake Bay during the third week in May and ceased operation at Morehead City, North Carolina, around December 23.

The Atlantic Fishing Company did not own any processing plants; therefore they had to sell their catch of menhaden fish to processing plants that were owned by other companies. Around 1960, the power block was introduced into the industry and the estimated cost per vessel for acquisition and installation was $250,000. The power blocks were hydraulic units using power from the main engine of the purse boats. This made it possible to use larger nets, and make the

A History of Colonna's Shipyard and Its People

Colonna's marine railway No. 4 was built in 1920. At that time it was the world's largest wooden railway and was capable of lifting five thousand tons. These images serve to illustrate the ability of the railway to lift and pull large vessels out of the water.

Painting of the steel tug Half Hitch.

operation faster. The operation could then be accomplished with eight fewer men. However, the Atlantic Fishing Company decided to sell their boats instead of making this large risky investment. The entire company was sold to Reedville Oil and Guano Company, Inc., of Reedville, Virginia, on December 27, 1961, for the amount of $500,000.

Menhaden fishing is always a big gamble. Fortunes have been made in one season and lost in the next. There is no exact way to predict the abundance of these fish at any season or for any area of the waters. About the only certainty in the business is that the men catching the fish with these boats and huge circling nets work long hard, seemingly endless hours under stressful conditions; however, when you stop to think about it, this is true with all men that work the waters for a living.

Norfolk Ship Salvage, Inc.

It was around 1947 that Norfolk Ship Salvage, Inc., which was owned and operated by B. O. Colonna Sr. and W. W. Colonna Sr., was formed. In the company's early years its primary activity was the scrapping of obsolete steam tugs and various small barges and cargo vessels that had been decommissioned following the end of World War II. The scrapping operation was begun after the vessels had been docked at Colonna's Shipyard. Often brass port lights, steering wheels, brass valves, and other parts were salvaged and either reused or sold. As time passed the scrapping of vessels became less lucrative and the tug and barge business grew, so eventually the name of the company was changed to Norfolk Towing and Lighterage, Inc. After a while the company sold its tugs and changed its name once again, this time to Norfolk Barge Company.

In its early years as Norfolk Ship Salvage, the company began operation with two wooden tugs, the *Michigan* and *J. C. Jr.*; one steel tug, the *Half Hitch*; and fourteen steel deck barges ranging in size from 110 to 130 feet long by 30 to 34 feet wide. During its tenure as Norfolk Towing and Lighterage, the company acquired the tug *Jack*, which was renamed the *Carl D. Colonna* and the tug *Iberia*, which was renamed the *Evelyn Colonna*. Both tugs were made of steel. The number of barges remained approximately the same as before. When the name was changed to Norfolk Barge, the company acquired one steel tug the *Easton*, which was renamed the *Will Colonna*. This tug had a twelve-hundred-horsepower Enterprise diesel engine making it the most powerful tug in the history of its fleet. During this era a couple barges were scrapped and several barges of similar size were purchased. Also a 90-foot-by-60-foot spud barge and the *Major Mud*, a mudscow were added to the fleet.

During the company's past, the tugs were mainly engaged in transporting sand, gravel, grain, oil and petroleum products, etc. mostly on a leased basis in the Hampton Roads, Eastern North Carolina, James River, and Chesapeake Bay areas. The barges were leased mostly for general cargo, marine contractors, and shipyard uses in the Hampton Roads area.

Benjamin Okeson Colonna Sr.

The year 1954, saw a change in the presidency of Colonna's Shipyard, Captain Will stepped down and in January 1954, his brother Benjamin Okeson Colonna Sr. became the third president of the shipyard. Captain Ben had actually assumed the duties of vice president in 1907 and continued in that capacity until becoming president.

Benjamin was born on January 14, 1887, in what was then known as the Colonna homestead (*Pescara*). It was an old farmhouse that had survived from

Benjamin Okeson Colonna Sr. in his office at Colonna's Shipyard.

the colonial era. Having been constructed around 1735 on what was known then as the Travis farm; in 1881 it became surrounded by a bustling shipyard that was built on the Eastern Branch of the Elizabeth River.

Benjamin as three of his brothers before him received his early education at the private school that was operated by the Reverend Robert Gatewood in Berkley. After completing the course of study offered at the Gatewood School,

Two of the Colonna brothers: Captain Will (left) and Captain Ben (right). Captain Will was president of the shipyard from 1907 until 1954. When this picture was taken in 1955, Ben was serving as president of Colonna's Shipyard.

Edward Holt Colonna, superintedent of cranes and other vehicles.

Benjamin received the rest of his formal education at the Norfolk Academy. During his boyhood years he spent his after-school hours and summer vacations at Colonna's Shipyard and at the age of eighteen, entered the business on a full-time basis. He served his apprenticeship as a ship carpenter, becoming familiar with all phases of operations in the ship repair industry, and eventually assumed responsibilities in general management. As previously mentioned Benjamin and two of his brothers assumed operation of the shipyard on a trial basis in 1907. Five years later they purchased the business from their father, Charles J. Colonna.

Captain Ben as he was better known was also president of Atlantic Fishing Company, a firm engaged in menhaden fishing in waters from Cape Fear, North Carolina, to Long Island, New York.

On January 5, 1909, Benjamin O. Colonna married Mary Glenn Perry of Okisko, North Carolina. The wedding took place at Tarboro, North Carolina.

The groom's brother, Edward Holt Colonna, and Miss Mabel E. Dalby of Norfolk accompanied the couple. Eventually Benjamin and Mary became the parents of one daughter, Glenn Perry Colonna, and one son, Benjamin Okeson Colonna Jr.

Captain Ben remained president of Colonna's Shipyard for fourteen years before resigning in 1968. His son Benjamin Jr. then succeeded him.

W. W. Colonna Jr. Remembers

Willoughby Warren Colonna Jr., better known as Bill, was born on February 1, 1929, in Norfolk Protestant Hospital. In 1936, in order to reflect the non-sectarian nature of the hospital, its name was changed to Norfolk General Hospital. Bill's parents were Willoughby Warren Colonna Sr. and Esther Pearl Daughtry Colonna. His paternal grandfather, Charles Jones Colonna, founded the shipyard in 1875.

Bill attended Campostella Heights Grammar School, Maury High School, and spent his senior year at Portlock High School where he graduated on June 10, 1947. After graduation, he attended the Norfolk Division of the College of William and Mary–VPI, now Old Dominion University, for one year and the Newport News Shipyard Apprentice School for one year. He also served a stint in the US Army at Fort Belvoir, Virginia.

At a very early age he helped his father pick-up scrap copper, lead, and brass at the shipyard. His first year on the payroll was around 1945. From 1943 to 1946, during his summer vacations from school, he worked as an outside machinist helper. That meant he carried the machinist's toolbox from job to job and helped him accomplish his many chores. Their work place was not only in the yard but was also on the vessels down at the pier. He recalls that it was a pretty hard job and was quite a learning experience. Back in those days workers spent most of their time on the job and learned a trade from an experienced mechanic.

After becoming a full-time employee, Bill did a rotation of the shipyard, working in most of the different trades, thus familiarizing himself with the various phases of operation before assuming increasing responsibility in several supervisory capacities. Eventually he went to the shipyard office where he first served as an assistant superintendent to Carl D. Colonna Jr., then superintendent, and in 1968 he became vice president, a position that he held for about ten years. During his supervisory rotation he received training from W. W. Colonna Sr., B. O. Colonna Sr., Carl D. Colonna Jr., and B. O. Colonna Jr., all capable and outstanding men in the shipyard business.

When asked, Bill will tell you that in today's world the shipyard is certainly a different place. In the earlier years the operation was smaller, it consisted of fewer people and they worked at a different pace. Also there were some trades back then, such as the ship carpenter and caulker that do not exist today. During World War II the yard was a busy place, but by 1945 things were beginning to wind down and the size of the work force had decreased from about 150 to 135 employees.

Prior to World War II there were only four or five people in the entire yard that had cars; so parking was not a problem like it is today. Fred Baker, an earlier employee, stated that when he first began working at the shipyard that some people rode horses to work, tied them to a post, fed them at lunch time, and of course rode them back home at the end of the workday. In those days most employees walked to work from the nearby communities of Berkley, Campostella, and even as far away as South Norfolk.

Bill's father, Captain Will Colonna Sr., and his Uncle, Captain Ben Colonna Sr., president and vice president, respectively, of the shipyard, shared an office and a large desk in the old office building. One sat on one side and the other sat on the opposite side of the same desk. At this particular time, Ben Jr., Carl Jr., and Bill Jr., the "Colonna boys" as they were known as, were asked to attend a meeting each Friday morning with Captains Will and Ben. At the first meeting the Colonna boys wanted to know what they were going to talk about. They were told, "Let's just talk about things and we will decide what we want to say as we go along." As these meetings went on they became more informative and the younger generation learned a lot about the operation of the shipyard from the two men who had been there since the very early years. In the beginning the boys didn't realize it but they were being groomed to take over the operation when Captains Will and Ben would no longer be available to share the real burdens of the business.

Payroll Change—Another Remembrance

Originally Colonna's, like most businesses at that time, paid their employees in cash. Each Friday afternoon someone went to the bank and brought the cash back to the yard in a cloth bag. The paymaster would then write the employee's name on the outside of an envelope and then place the amount due, in cash, inside. When the whistle blew the employees would line up at the pay window, give their name and receive their pay for the week. This weekly routine was no secret and many people knew about it.

On one occasion Captains Will and Ben heard that some people were planning to rob the shipyard of its payroll. So on the afternoon in question they placed armed people outside the gate, on top of the old machine shop building, and inside the office. Sure enough, before the whistle blew, a strange car with several occupants drove inside the shipyard, pulled up to the office and sat there for a few minutes. Then for no apparent reason they suddenly backed out and sped away. Most likely they saw the people on top of the machine shop and outside the gate and had second thoughts about trying to steal the payroll. After this occurrence, the two brothers began to consider making a change in the payroll process.

So, on May 2, 1955, a special meeting of both the stockholders and directors was held for the purpose of discussing and acting on a proposal to eliminate the method of cash payroll in favor of paying by check. The proposal received an affirmative vote by both and the method of paying the employees was changed from cash to check. At the meeting a motion was made by B. O. Colonna Sr. that a check-writing machine be purchased. The motion was passed and from that day forward payroll checks have been used instead of cash.

Pranksters of Sort

Bill Colonna remembers both his father Will and Uncle Ben as serious men of business; however, they were also known as pranksters and enjoyed a good laugh especially at the expense of others. So let's add a little humor to our story by exploring several of their escapades starting with the requirements of the ship carpenter.

The Ship Carpenter

The ship carpenter was a trade of the early ships and shipyards in the days of wooden vessels. It is quite possible that Colonna's was one of the last shipyards in the local port to employ ship carpenters. In those days Colonna's Shipyard purchased logs and processed them in its own sawmill. The ship carpenters would dress, plane, and shape the timbers as needed for the construction and repair of the many wooden vessels of the day. For the most part it is now a lost trade; however, on rare occasions the services of a ship carpenter may be needed in the building of a replica of a wooden sailing vessel. It was a trade that required a lot of talent and hard work.

Note all the logs in this aerial view of the shipyard in the late 1940s. The old Berkley bridge and coal pier can be seen in the upper right corner.

So, where did the Colonna brothers acquire the large number of logs needed for their operation? Captains Will and Ben usually purchased logs from one elderly gentleman. He would make his delivery, and then go to their office where after making himself comfortable on the sofa he would figure his bill. Having done this he would present it to the brothers who would then have the secretary prepare a check for payment of the logs. Captains Will and Ben would sign the check, give it to the man, and with payment in hand he would leave happy. This routine continued for many years.

Sometime later the brothers acquired an ignition coil from an old Ford automobile. The coil was capable of producing a lot of voltage but not much current, so while it wouldn't burn you it did have the ability to deliver a painful shock that would make an individual jump and momentarily act like a wild person. The brothers decided to rig the sofa with the ignition coil and naked wires. They ran the wires to the desk where they had installed a push button that enabled them to control the flow of current to the wires under the sofa cushion covers.

Eventually the elderly gentleman made another delivery of logs and as usual he went to the office, seated himself on the sofa, and began to figure the cost of the logs. Both Ben and Will were sitting at the desk. Ben looked over at Will and said, "I don't think I can help myself. I have to do something, not much but just a little something." He then proceeded to apply a short push of the button. The old gentleman jumped up, looked around, and didn't say anything but sat right back down. A few minutes passed and Ben said, "I can't help it, I just have to do it again, but this time I have to do it a little longer" and so he did. This time the man jumped up in the air, his pad went in one direction and his pencil in another. He went over, picked them both up, turned, faced the two men and said, "I guess you think that was real funny; well I tell it was not funny at all, this is the last time I will come in this office and also the price of logs has just gone up." The men may have enjoyed a good laugh at the expense of the old gentleman, but in the long run it cost them where it hurt the most and that was in the pocketbook.

You would think after having a few pranks fail that brothers Will and Ben would have had second thoughts before attempting others. However, that was not the case. By some hook or crook they acquired a female mannequin from a Norfolk department store and placed her in the men's room across the hall from their desk in the old office building. There she stood at the sink in all her glory wearing nothing but panties and bra and a towel draped around her arm. The brothers sat patiently waiting to see the reaction of the male workers as they entered the restroom. Invariably the reaction of each man was the same. They would take one or two steps into the men's room, see the woman, their faces would turn beet red and they would apologize, saying "I'm sorry, very sorry" several times while backing out the door. Meanwhile Will and Ben watching their reactions would almost crackup laughing.

The next story just goes to show you that most men never lose the thrill of seeing a beautiful woman. By this time both Captains Will and Ben were referred to as being very old in age—possibly octogenarians plus. They were seated at their desk minding their own businesses when this most beautiful well-developed secretary walked pass the door to their office. One said to the other, "Gosh if only I could be eighty-five again."

Chapter IV
1955–1980

Tug *Half Hitch*

This small steel tugboat, which was just forty-four feet in length was designed and built by Captains Will and Ben Colonna in 1957, for Norfolk Ship Salvage Company (later to become Norfolk Towing and Lighterage, Inc., and still later to become Norfolk Barge Company). The tug was equipped with a three-hundred-horsepower Caterpillar diesel engine. Its original purpose was to be used at the shipyard for shifting vessels around the railways and piers. However, a later decision was made to lease the tug to Hitch Sand and Gravel Company of Norfolk

The tug Half Hitch *shown here pulling a barge filled with sand, was designed and built by Captains Will and Ben Colonna in 1957. The small tug received its name from the Hitch Sand and Gravel Company that leased it from Colonna's Shipyard. It is now used at the shipyard for shifting vessels around the railways and docks.*

This photograph was taken of the vessel Charles J. Colonna *during its trial run in the 1950s.*

to be used for hauling sand and gravel from a point in the James River just beyond Hopewell to its plant south of the Gilmerton Bridge on the Southern Branch of the Elizabeth River south of the city of Norfolk. The small tug received its name from the sand and gravel company that it was leased to.

In 1964, the *Half Hitch* was placed on No. 3 Marine Railway at Colonna's Shipyard where it was cut in half, pulled apart and twelve feet was added to its mid-section. After expiration of its lease contract to the sand and gravel company the *Half Hitch* was returned to the shipyard where it is being used for its original purpose.

On Thursday June 29, 1961, Colonna's Shipyard was awarded a contract in the amount of $217,380 to convert three Navy landing crafts into ferryboats. The ferries were to be used by the state of North Carolina Highway Commission. Plans for the boats—two were to be placed in operation across Oregon Inlet and the other was to be used across Hatteras Inlet.

Benjamin Okeson Colonna Jr.

On February 6, 1968, Benjamin Okeson Colonna Jr. assumed the duties of president of Colonna's Shipyard. Ben Jr. had been born on April 18, 1922, and spent his early life living in the Campostella Heights section of the city of Norfolk, Virginia. When he was eighteen months old he was a prizewinner in a "Child Beauty Contest" and by the time he was about six, Ben would hop on his bike and pedal over to Colonna's Shipyard where his Uncle Will was president and his dad Benjamin Sr. was vice president. He loved hanging around the ships and the mechanics that worked on them and spent many of his summers at the yard.

At an early age, possibly around four or five years old, his parents received information that their young son was going to be kidnapped. As could be expected, this filled them with fear and they cautioned young Ben not to talk to any strangers and especially not to accept a ride with anyone that he did not know. A short time passed and one day while playing in front of his house and near the street a large black car pulled up near the curb, the windows had been rolled down and Ben saw that there were three men inside. One shouted, "Boy come here" as Ben approached the car, one of the men asked if he would like to go for a ride? Suddenly remembering the warnings from his parents, the young man turned and ran as fast as he could, probably to the back entrance of his home and reported the incident to either his mother or the maid Mammy Dolly.

It was at the age of ten that Ben first felt the thrill of sailing. He had learned the art of sailing and had gained experience in Pescara Creek that borders Colonna's Shipyard. Five years later his father bought him the first of several racing vessels and he began racing in competition at the young age of fifteen.

At the age of sixteen Ben served as an oiler on the Fishing Vessel *A. Brooke Taylor*, which operated out of the Taft Beach, Menhaden Company plant, in White Stone, Virginia.

In the summer of 1940 when he was eighteen years of age he decided to accept a job as a deck hand on the barge *Savannah*. The barge consisting of all wood timbers had been built in Maryland in 1912. She carried nine hundred tons of cargo and was used to transport packaged Domino sugar from the refinery in Philadelphia to Savannah and Brunswick, Georgia. The return cargo consisted of large rolls of paper pulp that was refined and made into paper products at a plant in Philadelphia.

Life aboard the *Savannah* was not easy and the food became monotonous, especially the breakfast meal. As the barge, which was towed by a small tug, passed through sections of North and South Carolina, Ben saw shanties of fishermen, built close to the canal banks, where they lived with their families under conditions that can only be described as abject poverty. The shanties were built of scrap lumber, tarpaper, tin, or whatever material they could find to use. The men made what living they could by fishing with long gill nets that they kept on homemade racks made of poles. Upon seeing the barge, the shabbily dressed children ran alongside for at least half a mile shouting, "throw me something." The members of the crew, having apples and oranges on board, would toss them to the hungry children.

About two weeks after leaving Norfolk, a stop was made at Charleston, South Carolina. Several members of the crew from the barge and the tug said they were going ashore and take liberty up town. Young Ben being tired of life on the barge asked if he could join them. Of course the old salts said yes and they all climbed into a rowboat and went ashore. It was not long before their journey took them to a place where they met several women. One of them asked Ben if he would like something to drink and he said that he would like an "orange crush." She laughed! Most likely there was none available. He soon noticed that his associates began disappearing, but that really did not concern him because he was enjoying the time away from the barge. However, the next day when they were back on the barge a light in his head clicked on and this naïve young man of eighteen realized that they had been in a house of ill repute and he later learned that the cost to each man was two dollars.

From Charleston they went to Savannah, Georgia. By that time, the weather was really getting hot. At some time in the past the deck of the barge had been completely covered with pitch and it was beginning to melt making the deck a sticky mess. It was like trying to walk on melted tar. To make walking a little easier the captain placed boards on the deck so the crew could walk without the feeling of being glued to the deck.

Soon after docking the longshoremen arrived and began to unload the barge. It took about two days to off-load the sugar cargo in Savannah before getting underway for Brunswick where they took on a load of paper pulp rolls and then departed for Philadelphia, Pennsylvania. After unloading the paper pulp into a warehouse the cycle began again starting with another load of Domino sugar. It took two eight-hour days to load the barge because the longshoremen did not work nights.

Once underway the next stop was Colonna's Shipyard. Ben had already told the captain that he would be leaving the barge because school would begin in ten days. From the shipyard Ben walked to his home in Campostella Heights where he met his mother. She was glad to see him even with his long hair and dark suntan. She immediately sent him upstairs to take a bath and change into clean clothes. The next trip was to the nearby branch of the Merchant and Planters Bank where Ben deposited $157.50, which represented two trips on the barge *Savannah* that lasted two and one half months. After leaving the bank, his mother took him to Patsy's Barber Shop in Berkley, where he got a haircut for twenty-five cents.

In June 1988 at the age sixty-six Ben sat and reminisced about that summer on the barge when he was just eighteen years old. He acquired a real education, he saw things that he had never seen before and had no idea existed. Having been raised as a child of privilege in a nice home he had never seen real poverty nor been exposed to hard work like he saw and experienced that summer almost fifty

This image of the barge Savannah *is among many paintings done by Casey Holtzinger for Colonna's Shipyard. Benjamin O. Colonna Jr. spent the summer of 1940 working on the* Savannah.

years earlier. It was an education that could not be learned in any formal school. The world at that time was also a better place. A person had more freedom and there were fewer government rules, regulations, and restrictions.

In 1941, Ben graduated from Maury High School in Norfolk, Virginia. His father wanted him to study medicine and become a doctor. He even arranged for Ben to accompany some doctors on their rounds, but he soon discovered that he could not stand the sight of blood. And so, instead, he began his career as an apprentice in the inside machine shop at Colonna's Shipyard at twenty-five cents per hour. Ben continued to maintain his interest in racing and even designed and built several boats himself. In 1945, his self-designed, self-built *Defender* defeated a field of eleven boats in the National Championship Regatta. He won two National Championships and one Governor's Cup, winning forty-one races in a row against some of the best sailors in the country.

By the age of twenty-four he had become an expert sailor, inside machinist, designer, superintendent, and boatbuilder. He had also won the heart and hand of Mildred McClellan and they were the proud parents of a one-year-old daughter, Carol, who would be their only child. In later years Carol became the bride of Henry Thomas Banks Jr. of Richmond, Virginia. Carol would later say that the shipyard was her father's life that he worked every day and a vacation was no longer than three days.

Carl Dunston Colonna Jr.

At the annual meeting of the Board of Directors of Colonna's Shipyard, which was held on February 2, 1972, President B. O. Colonna Jr. announced that Carl D. Colonna Jr. had requested retirement from the corporation. Carl had formerly served as first vice president and secretary of the shipyard. He had been employed at Colonna's for approximately forty-eight years; upon motion of B. O. Colonna Jr. and seconded by W. W. Colonna Jr. the vote was unanimous to accept his request.

Carl D. Colonna Jr. was born June 21, 1905; and. became actively employed by Colonna's Shipyard June 8, 1924, beginning in the paint shop and ascending to an executive position in January 1940.

At that time it was considered impossible for the shipyard to compensate its officers and directors for their extensive service rendered or to create and provide any retirement fund or plan for the benefit of its employees, including the officers and supervisory personnel. The members of the shipyard Board of Directors, however, did ask Carl D. Colonna Jr. to remain available as a consultant. In return he would receive $10,000 per year in equal weekly installments for the rest of his life. Upon Colonna's death his widow would receive a total sum of $5,000. In addition the shipyard maintained at its own expense life insurance coverage in the amount of $10,000. His official date of retirement was February 2, 1972.

As previously stated, on February 6, 1968, Benjamin O. Colonna Jr. became the fourth president of Colonna's Shipyard, succeeding his father who became co-chairman of the Board of Directors. Ben Jr. remained in the position of president until October 1977. When he made his departure, he told his cousin Bill Colonna, "All you are going to see of me is my coattail." This was certainly not an accurate prediction for he continued to maintain an office there and visited the yard not only on regular workdays, but also on Saturdays and Sundays and even on Christmas Day. Now there was a man that missed his job.

Carl D. Colonna Jr.

Benjamin Oakeson Colonna Jr.

W. W. Colonna Jr.—Fifth President

In his youth, Bill Colonna became widely known for his achievements in waterskiing, becoming the Virginia State waterskiing champion. His other sporting interest included boating, weight lifting, and body building; winning the title of Mr. Norfolk in 1955 and Mr. Virginia in 1957. When his father purchased an airplane for personal use and to maintain contact with the menhaden fishing industry, Bill went to the Glenrock Airport where at the age of seventeen he acquired a private pilot's license for single-engine land and also seaplanes. At that time he became the youngest person in the Commonwealth of Virginia to receive a seaplane rating. It has been said that he can also do a great impersonation of Al Jolson and in his early years appeared in local minstrel shows.

Upon purchasing the shipyard on October 17, 1977, W. W. Colonna Jr. (Bill) became its fifth president and chief executive officer. Under his management many changes have taken place. His predecessors tended to shy away from government work, and were satisfied for the yard to exist on commercial work, which amounted to an income of about $7 million annually. At that time the workload required the services of approximately 135 employees. Under his management, the number of employees soon quadrupled and the annual income increased sevenfold. W. W. Colonna Jr. remained in the position of president and chief executive officer until October 18, 1993, when he turned the reins over to Thomas W. Godfrey Jr.

Although long past the age when most people retire, he continues to show up for work each day. The younger people handle the day-to-day operation, however he is still available to make the larger more difficult decisions. Some of the more recent additions and improvements that have taken place during his reign include: the purchase of an eighteen-thousand-ton floating dry dock, a twenty-eight-hundred-ton floating dry dock, a 17-acre waterfront industrial site on Kimball Terrace in Norfolk that has been designated as a yacht yard, equipment and materials for construction of a large inside machine shop and heavy steel fabrication facility, and a three-story office building. Then there is the development of the West Yard, which includes two new piers, bulkheads, dredging, ground surface preparation and a one-thousand-metric-ton Marine Travelift with ten births for smaller vessels and barges. The most recent acquisition is a 7.4-acre waterfront industrial site and office building adjoining the West Yard at the foot of South Main Street in Berkley.

The Republic Seabee, which was the company aircraft, was capable of taking off and landing on either land or water. It was piloted by Bill Colonna when he was just seventeen years old.

He often looks out the windows of his new office on the third floor and comments about the growth, improvements, and value of the shipyard and in doing so he states, "We have certainly been fortunate."

Mr. Colonna is the father of three grown children and has nine grandchildren; some of them have a part in the operation of Colonna's Shipyard, thus hopefully assuring him that the family shipyard will continue for generations to come.

Willoughby Warren Colonna Sr.

Much has been written about the gentleman that was known most of his life as "Captain Will" and much more is needed to describe the man that lived his entire life along a mere three-mile section that extended from Colonna's Shipyard to his home in Oaklette. In his youth both were in Norfolk County. Today that distance stretches between the cities of Norfolk and Chesapeake, Virginia.

So why was he called Captain Will instead of just Will or Mr. Colonna? The term captain was an honorary title usually given to a person in charge, especially a person affiliated with boats or ships.

Captain Will was a rather small man, standing approximately five feet six inches and weighing in at about 165 pounds. He was the third of six sons and the fourth child of Charles Jones and Margaret Okeson Dunston Colonna. His siblings are addressed elsewhere in this history. Will was born on Monday, November 6, 1882, in the old colonial house that was on an existing farm bought by his father

Willoughby Warren Colonna Sr.

and uncle in September 1880. His Uncle Benjamin A. Colonna had named the nearby creek, house, and the rest of the property *Pescara*, a name that had been given to a Colonna stronghold many centuries earlier in Italy. The house, which had been built around 1735, stood at the head of what later became No. 2 railway in the shipyard. In later years, Captain Will's first two children, Fanny Mae and Dorothy Evelyn, were born in the same house and same room in which their father and three of their uncles had been born.

Early photographs show Will wearing skirts and sporting long blond curls. As a recorded story goes, when he was five years of age his sister Margaret Evelyn, who was just two years older, sat him in a high chair and proceeded to remove his long golden curls with a sharp pair of scissors. When his mother saw this she was shocked and began to cry. Nothing has been written about any punishment that his sister may have received for her actions. In later years, Evelyn, as she was known, remarked that his curls were the envy of many female relatives.

Willoughby Warren Colonna received his early education in Berkley at the private school of the Reverend Robert Gatewood and from there he became a student at Norfolk Academy where he not only excelled in academics but in athletics as well. He set several records in field and track, records that would remain unbeaten for many years to come.

After graduating from Norfolk Academy in 1902, Will attended the Virginia Polytechnic Institute (VPI) in Blacksburg, Virginia, where he was a member of the cadet corps and majored in mechanical engineering. He was very successful in all his studies; however, after two years at VPI and learning that his father was making plans to sell the shipyard, Cadet Will Colonna resigned and returned home.

Will along with his brothers Ben and Carl tried relentlessly to persuade their father to sell the business to them. As was mentioned earlier, in 1907, their father, Charles J. Colonna, agreed to put his sons to the test and if after a period of five years they proved to him that they could operate the shipyard successfully and show a continuous profit, he would sell them the business.

So in 1907, Charles abated his involvement in the business and let the three young men have a go at running the operation. Will, assumed the duties of president, Ben as vice president, and Carl as secretary and treasurer. Their father remained on the Board of Directors where he was able to keep an eye on the performance of his sons. The five years passed and Charles' sons had done well at operating the shipyard. In 1912, he decided to sell the business to the three of them and retire to his home on Colonial Avenue in Norfolk, Virginia. Will, continued as president, Ben as vice president, and Carl as secretary and treasurer.

The Colonna brothers Will, Ben, and Carl were working in the shipyard one day in the early 1900s when this beautiful car drove up. Its owner parked the car and walked down to a boat tied at a pier. The brothers greatly admired this dream car. They ran home and changed from their work clothes into their finest, then had a workman snap this picture posed in the car. Then they hurriedly jumped out of the car and changed back into their work clothes. The owner never knew about their fun with his car.

In 1920, things were going well at the shipyard and Captain Will and his brothers installed the world's largest wooden railway. It was a forty-five-hundred-ton marine railway capable of lifting most of the world's vessels at that time. Its capacity was later increased to five thousand tons.

It was also in 1920 that Captain Will Colonna designed and built his dream home on a twenty-acre point of land overlooking the Indian River, a part of the Eastern Branch of the Elizabeth River in the Oaklette section of Norfolk County. Its location was about three miles east of the shipyard. Will kept his yacht the *Margaret*, which was named for his mother, moored at his pier at Oaklette where it caught fire, burned to its waterline, and sank across the river in a small cove. Additional information about the Colonna house can be found in Chapter IX of this history.

Around 1927, Captain Will assisted by his young daughters built a houseboat on an existing Chesapeake and Ohio wooden railroad pontoon, which probably dated back to the early 1900s. The houseboat was built as a hunting lodge. A full description of the houseboat and its hunting trips are covered in Chapter IX.

On March 20, 1961, Will's second wife Esther Pearle Daughtry Colonna, mother of Bill and Caroline, passed away at the age of sixty years. After that Captain Will lived the rest of his life at 831 St. Lawrence Avenue where he enjoyed visits from family and friends. In the fall of each year it gave him great pleasure to collect pecans from the 101 trees that he had planted around 1920. Part of his relaxation came from raking and burning the leaves dropped by the trees on the land where his dream house once stood. He also enjoyed reading detective stories, putting picture puzzles together, and loved reading and writing poetry. He played rummy with anyone who would dare play with him because it has been said that he was hard to beat.

Will was born in the slower world of the horse and buggy and even saw streetcars that were pulled by horses and later were moved by electricity from an overhead wire and trolley. He lived through the industrial revolution of the 1920s; experienced the life of living in a large mansion, owning a sixty-five-foot yacht, driving the earlier as well as later model automobiles. He saw the invention and development of the airplane, electric lights, the telephone, and television. He even lived to see a man land on the moon. He worked on wooden ships that received their power from wind and sails, then ships of steel that operated from steam, diesel- and finally nuclear-powered vessels. In his early life there was little government control and few taxes. He later saw much government control and high taxes, which he hated until the day he died.

Chapter V

1980–2000

USS *Fortify*—Navy Minesweeper

After fifteen years of sticking to repairs of commercial vessels, the officials at Colonna's Shipyard decided in January 1984 to resume bidding on Navy ship repairs. After all, the market for commercial jobs had become very depressed and there was not much of that type of work available.

The nation had hit an industrial slump and there was a glut of oil which resulted in less petroleum being carried along its waterways, so barge owners were putting most of their dollars into their larger vessels instead of into barges and tugs. This hurt Colonna's and other yards that specialized in repairing barges and tugboats. Adding to Colonna's problem was the fact that larger shipyards had begun to seek small ship repairs that they had previously ignored.

Aerial view of the shipyard on April 11, 1984.

Military Sealift Command's cable laying/repair ship USNS Zeus *at the shipyard in 1994. In October 2010 Colonna's Shipyard was again awarded a contract for regular overhaul of the USNS Zeus, which included dry-docking and undocking the ship; work on the main propulsion motors; transducer and sonar equipment installation; underwater hull preservation; and propulsion shaft removal and inspection.*

The shipyard that had been founded by Charles J. Colonna in 1875 and run by members of the family since, invested more than $1 million in new facilities, equipment, and services to prepare for the possible return of Navy work. The Navy contract for $1.53 million that was eventually awarded to Colonna's was small by Navy standards but it turned out to be the most important job the shipyard had done for some time. On May 15, 1984, the USS *Fortify*, a Navy minesweeper came into Colonna's Shipyard for overhaul. In addition to the minesweeper the yard also received a job to overhaul a Navy tug amounting to a $732,000 contract that grew into $1.1million when the Navy approved additional repairs. The work on the tug was completed in July 1984.

The minesweeper *Fortify* was kind of like a throwback to earlier days of the shipyard. Its hull was not made of steel. It was made of wood—fir and oak—in order to make it less vulnerable to magnetic mines. The earlier wooden ships were the heydays of caulkers and ship carpenters. The caulkers took mauls and drove cotton and hemp into seams where water could possibly seep in through a ship's hull. The ship carpenter spent more time shaping wood than mauling it.

This was not the first federal government work that Colonna's was involved in. In early 1924, the shipyard branched out into government work and was awarded a contract to build ten fast boats for the US Coast Guard to use in enforcing the national prohibition laws. As previously noted, the first boat, CG-223, was launched on October 6, 1924.

More Navy Contracts

In December 1984, the *Tidewater Digest* reported that Colonna's Shipyard, Inc., of Norfolk topped the list of recipients of recent contract awards by the Navy's Supervisor of Shipbuilding, Conversion, and Repair in Portsmouth. Colonna's won an $878,000 contract to overhaul a floating crane and a $265,000 job to make miscellaneous repairs to the *Saipan*, an amphibious assault ship.

In August 1985, Colonna's Shipyard was awarded a $3.1 million contract to make structural, piping, and mechanical repairs to the Navy barge *UEB-1*. It was at that time, the largest Navy contract in the company's history. The barge *UEB-1* was used in various Navy experiments. Work began in January 1986 and was completed in April of the same year.

Coast Guard Ship Repairs

In August 1986, information received by Colonna's was that they were apparently the lowest bidder on a job to overhaul two Coast Guard cutters, but would have to await a Navy inspection before the formal contract could be awarded. The work was to be on Coast Guard ships but the Navy would be the administrator of the contract.

At this same time Colonna's was in the middle of a $9 million expansion. A major part of that expansion was to include the 620-foot floating dry dock that was to arrive from Rotterdam, Holland, later in the month.

On Tuesday, September 9, 1986, Senator John Warner's office announced that Colonna's Shipyard would get $12 million for overhauling two Coast Guard cutters, each 210 feet long, and would have options on similar work for nine more of the vessels. The total bid on the eleven ships was $62.7 million. It was the biggest job in the shipyard's 111-year history.

Eventually the cutters *Courageous* and *Durable* came to the yard and work

On Sunday September 28, 1986, against the backdrop of downtown Norfolk's increasing skyline, the Mighty Servant 3 is seen passing through the Berkley Bridge on its way to delivering a floating dry dock to Colonna's Shipyard.

was begun. Later, on Friday, June 24, 1988, the shipyard suspended repairs on the two Coast Guard cutters and as a result was forced to layoff 250 of its 850 employees. The reason behind those actions—the corporation had not been paid for millions of dollars' worth of repairs that had been performed on the ships. The paperwork began to fly between the shipyard and the Navy. It was not long before an agreement was reached between Colonna's and the Navy which called for the shipyard to resume work on the ships, however, it would take time to recall the 250 workers that had been laid off. This would eventually be the straw that broke the camel's back for as we will see later it led Colonna's Shipyard into Chapter 11 bankruptcy.

Floating Dry Dock (The Captain Will)

Prior to 1986, the officers and directors of Colonna's Shipyard began searching for a floating dry dock. The search, which was conducted by W. W. Colonna III, not only included the United States, but also included continental Europe and areas adjacent to the Mediterranean Basin, as well. Finally an eighteen-thousand-metric-ton dry dock was located in Amsterdam, Holland. A special meeting of

After leaving Rotterdam, Holland, encountering a hurricane, and spending about twelve days crossing the Atlantic, the Mighty Servant 3, *the world's largest semi-submergible ship, arrived at Colonna's Shipyard on September 28, 1986. Here it can be seen off-loading its cargo, a floating dry dock.*

Colonna's Board of Directors was held and it was decided to make a monetary offer and begin negotiations, which led to the purchase of the dry dock.

At the same meeting a resolution was approved relative to requesting the Bank of Virginia to grant a loan of $9 million to be used for the purchase of the dry dock in Amsterdam, the construction of a concrete mooring pier for the dry dock and other associated facility improvements necessary for the use of the floating dry dock and its certification.

Colonna's tentatively agreed to buy the dry dock from a city-owned shipyard in Amsterdam; however, the purchase was subject to the dock being towed to Rotterdam for an out-of-water inspection. Robert A. Coates, an engineer employed by Crandall Dry Dock Engineers, performed an inspection of floating dry dock No. 5 while it was moored at its berth in Amsterdam and reported that all readings indicated that it was in very good condition and would appear to be a sound investment. After the inspection at Rotterdam, Mr. Coates gave his final approval and the dry dock was purchased for the sum of $1.85 million. About three or four weeks later the dock was loaded on the *Mighty Servant 3* and began its journey to Colonna's Shipyard in Norfolk, Virginia.

Unfortunately, a bad hurricane was encountered during the trip and although the dry dock was damaged, Colonna's Shipyard received its first floating dry dock on Sunday, September 28, 1986. A.D.M. Shipyard of Amsterdam, Holland, had built the dry dock twenty-two years earlier. The crossing of the Atlantic Ocean on board the cargo deck of the *Mighty Servant 3*, the world's largest semisubmersible heavy lift vessel, took approximately twelve days. The construction of the dry dock was all welded steel, it was total electric, and had been in fresh water all of its life. The steel dry dock measures 620 feet in length, is 118 feet wide, and has a capacity to lift vessels weighing up to twenty thousand tons. It is equipped with a fifteen-ton crane on each wing wall, a pressure water wash system, and a trolley system for precise positioning of vessels in the dock. Articulated manlifts run the entire length of the wing walls to facilitate work on the sides of vessels. So how and where was it off-loaded upon arrival? The *Mighty Servant 3* was lowered by the opening of valves to admit water, causing the ship to submerge, after which tugboats gently nudged the floating dry dock off to one side. When the dry dock was successfully off-loaded, water was pumped out of the ship, causing it to rise back to its proper level. The floating dry dock was moored in Pescara Creek for approximately three months before going to Baltimore for repair of damages caused by the hurricane. After off-loading the dry dock the *Mighty Servant 3* made preparations to return home by way of Nova Scotia. The new floating dry dock, which was named for Captain Will Colonna became operational in May 1987.

Norfolk Barge Company

At this time, the company trading as Norfolk Barge Company, which had its beginning as Norfolk Lighterage Company and then became Norfolk Towing and Lighterage Company, had been a trusted source of deck barges and other floating equipment for a number of years. An experienced staff is available to help the customer select the right type of equipment needed for a specific job.

In January 1987, a meeting of the officers and directors of Norfolk Barge Company was held and it was decided to build a fourteen-thousand-foot metal building on property formerly owned by Prime Drum Corporation and located at the southeast corner of the intersection of Indian River Road and the Norfolk and Western Railroad tracks. The approximately cost of the building and associated property improvements would amount to about $500,000. The building would be leased to Colonna's Shipyard, Inc., for storage purposes.

Second Major Shipyard Threat

By 1990, the shipyard that had been a fixture along the waterfront of the Berkley section of Norfolk for 115 years, found itself struggling, and by April had no choice but to seek federal bankruptcy protection. So what happened? As mentioned earlier, hoping to boost the shipyard workload in the late 1980s, management embarked on an ambitious program to overhaul US Coast Guard cutters. This program was quite different from the yard's traditional work that had previously been on private tugs, barges, and small ships. Colonna's bid on and won a contract to overhaul eleven of the 210-foot-long cutters. However, when the specifications were received from the customer they were not clear at all. They were written so no one could understand them. The drawings and parts furnished by the Navy, who was managing the contract, did not match nor did they fit the ships. Needless to say this caused a tremendous loss in labor hours and other problems that bled the yard of an estimated $12 million on the two cutters that it did manage to complete.

The contract turned into a real disaster and to add insult to injury there was this woman politician who represented Baltimore in the House of Representatives. She made frequent visits to all the shipyards in Maryland and by doing so she became very popular and gained a lot of prestige. She proceeded to encourage the US government to open a small shipyard for the Coast Guard in Curtis Bay, Maryland. She was successful and the government immediately took the other nine vessels from Colonna's Shipyard and sent them to Curtis Bay.

Eventually $5.7 million was recovered from the US Navy and that was only after finding a little-known law where the Secretary of the Navy could award up to $25 million to anyone who had been treated unfairly by actions of the Navy.

Throughout the years the shipyard had occasionally faced hard times but nothing like this. It was the worst of times. To make ends meet the workload was halved. Revenues had been around $51.5 million in 1988; however, in 1991, they were down to $21.7 million. The workforce that had been almost nine hundred in 1988 was down to three hundred at that time.

Dry Dock Accident

To add to the existing problems, in October 1990, when the shipyard was trying desperately to obtain revenue to pay off its debts a dry dock accident occurred that caused almost three months loss of income. Colonna's workers were testing a dry dock's ability to take on a ship by lowering it into the water. The test, which is known as full submergence testing, consists of ballasting the dry dock to its lowest depth. This is accomplished by opening the flood valves thus allowing water from the river to flood into the pontoon tanks. The weight of the water then causes the dock to lower below the surface of the surrounding water and settle into the dredged basin. While normally all goes well, the sequence of events involved can be tricky and requires the work of experienced personnel.

Unfortunately and unbeknown to any of the workers there had been an underwater mudslide resulting in a filled-in corner of the dredged basin. When the dry dock was near its full submergence depth the bottom of the northwest corner struck this uplift that had been caused by the mudslide and the dock that had been level suddenly tilted causing the opposite corner to submerge. This allowed salt water from the Elizabeth River to flood the machinery spaces resulting in a total loss of power. This meant the pumps could not operate and the valves could not be closed. In less than fifteen minutes the weight of the rushing water into the machinery spaces caused the entire east wing wall to become submerged in seven feet of water.

However, the dry dock was designed so half of the machinery spaces, which include the pumps, valves, and piping, were installed in each wing wall. This meant that one wing wall was still above water and half of the main pumps and valves were still accessible. With the assistance of personnel from Colonna's Dry Dock and Engineering Departments and those from Crofton Diving Company the effort to raise the dry dock was begun. The divers went about sealing openings in the submerged east wing wall, barges with generators were brought in to power the pumps and control some valves, the engineers established pumping amounts for each tank and after many long and difficult hours the dock was finally out of the water.

This was not the end for much work of a different kind had to be accomplished. All areas that had been under salt water had to be flushed with fresh water, all removable parts such as pumps, valves, motors, etc., were removed, cleaned, and replaced.

The dry dock was eventually removed from its mooring and dredging was performed to remove the accumulation caused by the mudslide. After this was complete the dock was reinstalled.

This major accident that occurred in the middle of October took until late December to make the necessary repairs and to get the dry dock fully recertified by government inspectors, all at a cost of $3 million. By this time the Jonathan Corporation, which had leased the dry dock from Colonna's, stopped making rent payments. Eventually the two companies did renegotiate a new lease agreement.

Bankruptcy

Many people think that bankruptcy is just a matter of filing a piece of paper and after that you are free of debt—that there is no cost involved. It is really not quite that simple especially if it is a business that is filing; however, Federal bankruptcy laws do provide a legal procedure by which a debtor may obtain some measure of relief from the demands of creditors. Different types of bankruptcy are referred to by chapter numbers of the Federal Bankruptcy Code. Chapter 11 is used primarily by businesses. Under a Chapter 11 proceeding, the debtor negotiates with creditors to reduce the amount he owes them or to extend the amount of time he has to repay them. While the plan is being put together, all efforts to collect money from the debtor are prohibited, and after the plan is approved, all of the creditors named in the petition are bound to it.

An officer or trustee appointed by the court to oversee the operation of the business during the period of bankruptcy can result in considerable cost. That person usually requires a large salary plus many other benefits such as receiving a percentage of any profits, bonuses, and payment of membership dues in professional organizations, a personal car, and much more.

Then an Advisory Board of Directors may be developed by a management company which charges a large fee and each member of the Board may receive several hundred dollars for every meeting attended. As you can see bankruptcy is not cheap. So what happens next? The next major hurdle to be cleared is approval of the reorganization plan.

Approval of Reorganization Plan

On Wednesday, November 13, 1991, US Bankruptcy Court Judge Hal Bonney Jr. approved Colonna's reorganization plan. It was the final act in a twenty-month courtroom drama, which put the city's oldest shipyard against many of its longtime bankers, suppliers, and subcontractors. Under terms of the reorganization, the shipyard was faced with writing some big checks in the upcoming winter months, and those checks were to be followed by regular payments over the following ten years. The plan was to repay all of the shipyard creditors by December 31, 2001.

During much of this time an interim team of outside managers ran the shipyard. On November 13, 1991, the day the corporation won court approval for bankruptcy reorganization, this team of managers was dismissed, for they had served their purpose. Also on November 13, W. W. Colonna Jr. returned to the shipyard after, at the advice of his attorney, having stayed away for a period of two months. The employees had posted a sign at the shipyard entrance that stated, "Welcome Home Bill Colonna Jr." The very appreciative proprietor of Colonna's Shipyard stopped his pickup truck, climbed in its back and talked to all the employees that met him at the gate. Stop and think about it. Here was a sixty-two-year-old man, the age when most men are thinking about retirement, embarking on what could be considered the beginning of a new career. The general opinion at that time was that the shipyard, because of its previous temporary management, had reached the lowest point in its many years of operation.

After a long spell of financial woes, including twenty months under Chapter 11 bankruptcy protection, the shipyard in Berkley began to receive a sizable amount of work and by November 1992, the dry docks were booked until July of the following year.

Thomas W. Godfrey Jr., who had served in company finance and administration for a number of years, now as president/CEO of Colonna's Shipyard, would help lead the company out of the bankruptcy years. Also at that time, W. W. Colonna III assumed the position of vice president.

Sometime later, to everyone's surprise, a letter was received from the Navy Department stating that in fact they had been unfair in their dealings with Colonna's Shipyard. But their admission still did not change the amount of the award that had been requested.

This photograph taken on April 5, 1968, shows the steam yacht Dauntless *undergoing sea trials after having received a complete overhaul at Colonna's Shipyard.*

Third Major Shipyard Threat

A third possible shipyard threat is what is referred to as "death taxes." This is what could possibly happen to a business the size of Colonna's Shipyard; at the death of the owner. To begin with the Internal Revenue Service would have the shipyard appraised, a small amount of the appraised value would be considered tax-free and the remaining amount would then be taxed at the rate of 55 percent. This would put the yard in such a position that most likely it would not be able to survive and after all these many years, it would have no alternative but to close or be sold. At this time shipyard attorneys are challenging the laws governing this procedure. After all, the members of the Colonna family, beginning with Charles J. back in 1875, have always paid their fair share of taxes. Why should they be treated so unfairly?

Yacht *Delphine*/USS *Dauntless*

Before the division of Colonna Yachts was formed, the Main Yard occasionally repaired or even overhauled a yacht, which helped to supplement its income from

commercial and military contracts. One such yacht was the *Delphine/Dauntless*. The yacht *Delphine* was built in 1921 by the Great Lakes Engineering Works of Detroit, Michigan, for the Dodge family of automobile makers. Most of its early years were spent plowing the waters of the Great Lakes. In January 1942, the United States having entered World War II in December 1941, requisitioned the *Delphine*, changed its name to the *Dauntless* and made it the flagship for Admiral Ernest J. King, Chief of Naval Operations (CNO).

After World War II, the vessel was returned to the Dodge estate and once again it became known as the *Delphine*. In 1967, the Seafarers Union along with several shipping companies purchased it for use by the Lundeberg Maryland Seamanship School, which was based at Piney Point, Maryland. At that time the name was again changed to the more masculine sounding name of *Dauntless*.

On December 21, 1967, the *Dauntless* began its journey to Colonna's Shipyard where it received a complete overhaul, including installation of new heating and plumbing systems, conversion of passenger to crew quarters, and refurbishing of her drawing, dining, and music rooms. After completion, the ship began sea trials on April 5, 1968.

After having several owners, in 1997 it became the property of the Bruynooghe family and underwent a six-year restoration; after which it served as a chartered cruise ship in the Mediterranean.

Colonna Yachts—A Division of Colonna's Shipyard

In the early 1990s the shipyard being faced with declining Navy contracts and a bout with bankruptcy realized it needed to seek different avenues of approach toward gaining new business. It's true that the Main Yard had long

The motor yacht Jamaica Bay *is one of many that have received service and repairs by Colonna Yachts. This photograph was taken at Colonna Yachts in April 2000.*

been repairing an occasional yacht, but actually there were limited facilities on the East Coast for the repair and service of mega-yachts, those in excess of 120 feet in length.

Colonna's had acquired a growing reputation in the yacht repair business and the time seemed right to establish what might be considered a world-class facility in Hampton Roads. A third of the world's largest yachts were in North America and most of them were on the East Coast. Yachts large and small travel both north and south on the Intracoastal Waterway. The waterway's midpoint zero-mile marker is in the Elizabeth River between Norfolk and Portsmouth.

By 1997, Colonna's was actively seeking and getting more yacht work. While the customers were pleased with the workmanship, they were not all that pleased with the surroundings of the main shipyard on the Eastern Branch of the Elizabeth River along Indian River Road. They were use to spending most of the year touring spiffy Mediterranean ports and other places where great wealth was obvious.

They were not comfortable being laid-up alongside dirty old barges and tugboats. So the search was on to find a more pleasing location. It was felt that a satellite yard away from the main shipyard would be the answer and the end result would be an increase in yacht work.

In 1963, the Norfolk Shipbuilding and Dry dock Corporation (Norshipco) was operating what was known as their Southern Plant—a small boat and yacht yard at 2401 Kimball Terrace within site of the Campostella Bridge in Norfolk, Virginia. The yard had been abandoned for some time. It was equipped with a marine railway capable of pulling large yachts from the water in order that complete hull work could be accomplished. The officers at Colonna's after careful investigation felt that with a significant amount of clean-up and restoration that the once active yard would be the perfect location for yacht repairs and service. Colonna's looked into acquiring the defunct Southern Plant from Norshipco and ultimately closed on the property in August 1998.

This new endeavor brought a different flavor to the shipyard's normal environment, which at the time consisted mostly of barges and tugboats. The luxurious boats or megayachts as they are often called brought a whole new line of work to Colonna's Shipyard. Some of these yachts are worth more than $50 million and include the latest in electronic equipment, and hundreds of thousands of dollars worth of crystal and china. Many of the yachts coming to the yard fly the flag of foreign nations making an understanding of perhaps French, Spanish, Arabic, or other languages a real asset.

Colonna Yachts offers a wide range of services. It refits boats that have changed ownership by customizing the interior and making other major changes. It repairs piping, electrical, and also mechanical systems. It also modifies boats. It has even extended the hull of some and by doing so, changing the lines of the vessel. On at least one occasion a yacht was refitted with a basketball court.

Needless to say, it takes big bucks to own a megayacht. Their owners are among the world's richest people. For example, the fuel tank may hold about twenty thousand gallons. Some of the yachts may require a fifteen-person crew and its repair or maintenance bills can run into millions of dollars. The larger yachts usually consist of three decks. The lower decks house the crew and machinery, while the owner's suite, guest cabins, saloon, and dining room are located on the main deck.

Popular destinations of these luxury vessels can run from the Mediterranean to New England to the Caribbean.

Chapter VI
2000–2011

Steel America

Steel America, a division of Colonna's Shipyard, Inc., was established in 2000 and specializes in heavy machining, fabrication, and repair. In addition Steel America supports ship repair, maintenance, and overhaul markets that require steel, stainless steel, or aluminum as materials of construction. They are able to support both small and large projects up to one thousand tons.

Throughout its history Colonna's Shipyard has repaired a variety of ships beginning with those powered by sail, then those powered successively by steam, diesel, and then nuclear. The two ships in this photograph, which was taken on September 9, 2006, are left to right: the Savannah which was the first nuclear-powered commercial ship in the world and the John W. Brown, a Liberty Ship from World War II.

Steel America, a division of Colonna's Shipyard is highly involved in the repair of propulsion shafts. This photograph which was taken April 27, 2010, of the inside machine shop shows work being accomplished on a sixty-two-ton shaft.

Here we see a machinist working on a US Navy propulsion shaft in the inside machine shop, October 2010.

In February 2009, the US Navy officially certified Steel America as an approved propulsion shaft repair facility. As a result of three years work involving several individuals from the inside machine shop and the Quality Assurance Department, on March 30, 2009, the facility was awarded a Basic Ordering Agreement (BOA). The BOA is a five-year contract to perform "Class A" repairs to Navy surface fleet propulsion shafts.

In April 2009, a newly acquired lathe, which will be of help in servicing the larger propulsions shafts, arrived at the inside machine shop. The lathe is computer controlled, has a chuck that is 10 feet in diameter and a bed that is 132 feet long. However, before this very large piece of equipment can be fully utilized, it will be necessary to enlarge the building. Shipment of the lathe was by truck from San Diego, California.

Flow Control Technologies

Flow Control Technologies, a division of Steel American and Colonna's Shipyard, is involved in the water and wastewater treatment industries. Their customers include those that are involved in water supply, flood control, hydroelectric plants, dams, and filtration plants, wastewater treatment facilities such as sewage treatment plants and sewage holding facilities.

Flow Control produces, among other things, cast-iron and stainless-steel sluice gates, stainless and aluminum slide gates, various types of valves, and stainless steel pipe for oxidizing or odor control air flow.

Down River

Colonna Down River Division is a mobile, full-service marine repair contractor that specializes in ship repair. It consists of a skilled and qualified workforce that represents the full spectrum of marine trades. A short-notice, rapid-response staff of professionals is available twenty-four hours a day 365 days a year. Also, the services of a complete inside machine shop and high-capacity steel fabrication shop are available.

Ocean Tech Services, formerly a separate division, has been dissolved and is now a part of Colonna Down River.

Trade Team

Trade Team, a division of Colonna's Shipyard, Inc., was founded in 2005. The idea behind its formation was to find the most talented trades people in the marine industry and to provide their services not only to Colonna's Shipyard and its divisions but to also extend their services to other companies as well. Among the skill trades provided are welders, ship fitters, pipe fitters, electricians, machinist, blasters/painters, hydro blasters, millwrights, riggers, and other specialized trades.

The *General Hoyt S. Vandenberg*

The *Vandenberg* actually began its long history as the *General Harry Taylor*. General Taylor, the man, commanded the US Ninth Air Force in Europe during World War II. The US Army later commissioned the ship as a transport vessel. In 1944, it ferried troops and supplies from San Francisco to island bases in the western Pacific Ocean.

In 1945, near the end of World War II it was used to bring troops home from Europe. Later the US Navy used it as a transport ship. In 1956, after the Soviet crackdown, it carried Hungarian freedom fighters to Australia. In 1961, the ship was transferred to the US Air Force. At that time it was renamed the *Vandenberg*. Later it was converted to track missile tests and followed the Mercury and Gemini space liftoffs. It even appeared in *Virus*, a 1999 science-fiction movie starring Jamie Lee Curtis, Donald Sutherland, and William Baldwin. In preparation for the movie, the ship was brought to Colonna's Shipyard where it received a major facelift to make it look like a Russian research vehicle. Along with the *Vandenberg*, Colonna's made over two tugboats to give them a Russian look. The tugboats were also used in the movie. Filming took place mainly off Cape Charles, in Newport News, and off Lambert's Point in Norfolk.

The General Hoyt S. Vandenberg, *formerly the* General Harry Taylor, *had a long history dating back to World War II. It made several trips to Colonna's Shipyard. This one was in 1997. Its last trip to the yard was in 2007.*

After serving as a missile tracker throughout the Cold War, the *Vandenberg* was retired in 1983 and joined the "Ghost Fleet" in the James River. It sat there alongside other obsolete and rusting vessels for about twenty-four years. In 2007, the US Maritime Administration gave it to the state of Florida to be used as an artificial reef. At that time the ship was towed to Colonna's Shipyard where cleanup to remove contaminants was accomplished.

The ship was scheduled to be sunk off Key West, Florida, in April 2008; but the City of Key West had trouble raising the necessary funds and the *Vandenberg* sat at Colonna's Shipyard as lawyers fought in federal court over unpaid bills amounting to more than $1.6 million. A federal judge ordered the ship to be sold at auction. When the auction was held on the steps of the Norfolk Federal Courthouse in December 2008, the price of steel had decreased and the sale brought only $1.35 million. The purchaser was a bank that was representing the City of Key West.

In January 2009, the *Vandenberg* was still docked at Colonna's. Eventually it was moved and arrived in Key West on April 22, 2009. At that time crews began working to prepare the ship for sinking on Wednesday May 27, 2009. The ship was sunk seven miles off Key West where it became one of the world's largest man-made reefs.

US Navy Warships

In January 2009, three US Navy Ships, the USS *Elrod* (FFG-55), the USS *Thunderbolt* (PC-12), and the USS *Freedom* (LCS 1) were dry-docked at Colonna's Shipyard.

The *Freedom*, which is one of the US Navy's newest littoral combat ships, is capable of reaching speeds in excess of forty-five knots and can obtain a range of three thousand nautical miles at sixteen knots. It is very maneuverable in that it can accelerate from zero to forty-plus knots in less than two minutes, decelerate from forty-plus to zero knots in approximately three ship lengths, and can move directly sideways at one knot. The *Freedom* also has the ability to rotate 360 degrees in about three minutes time. Littoral combat ships can be used in mine warfare, antisubmarine warfare, and surface warfare and also have the potential for other missions.

For over a year Colonna's Shipyard was involved with Lockheed Martin and others in providing quality repairs and maintenance to the new littoral combat

This photograph of the USS Freedom, *the Navy's first littoral combat ship, was taken at Colonna's Shipyard in January 2010.*

Three important ladies, left to right: Karen Colonna; Commander Kris Doyle, commanding officer of the USS Freedom; *and Evelyn Colonna. This picture was taken in March 2009 in the lobby of Colonna's office building.*

ship. On January 20, 2010, Colonna's was the recipient of a special recognition in the form of a selected framed photograph from Lockheed Martin for the work accomplished on LCS 1, USS *Freedom*. This presentation is indicative of the mutual respect and goodwill that has evolved through Colonna's partnership with Lockheed Martin.

When the *Freedom* arrived on January 12, 2009, the commanding officer was Commander Donald D. Gabrielson and the executive officer was Commander Kristy D. Doyle. On Saturday March 14, 2009, at 10:00 a.m., while still at the shipyard, a change of command ceremony was held onboard the *Freedom*. Commander Doyle relieved Commander Gabrielson. After the ceremony, a reception was held on the first floor of the new Colonna office building.

Shipyard's Expansion Plans

The old machine shop influenced the architectural design of Colonna's new office building.

Plans for the expansion of the shipyard included not only the West Yard, but also construction of a three-story office building to house the administrative offices. By January 2008, construction of a new office building immediately north of the existing main office was underway. The new tilt-slab concrete building is 80 by 132

Colonna's new office building was under construction in 2008 and some final touches were added in early 2009. This photograph was taken from across Pescara Creek and shows the back of the building.

A History of Colonna's Shipyard and Its People

Classroom in Colonna's office building.

The boardroom in Colonna's new office building.

feet and provides about 32,000 square feet of interior space. The architectural style is partly derived from the old inside machine shop with concrete walls, large windows, and pediment-type end walls. The entire shipyard and a part of the community of Berkley can be seen from the windows of the third floor.

Construction of the new office complex was a very significant undertaking in the history of the corporation, for an office building that would be dedicated to that purpose had never been built. Prior to occupation of the new structure the main office was located in a building that had been built in the 1920s, for service as a production mold loft.

The new building became home to many of the offices that were formally operating from temporary trailer or modular type buildings. This new special-purpose building supports the management and administrative activities of the shipyard and some of its divisions.

Shipyard Bell

Shortly after completion of the new office building a mounting post for the shipyard bell was installed in one corner of its lobby. The brass bell had been manufactured in 1854 at the Meneely Bell Foundry in Troy, New York, and in earlier years had seen service on the Graves Shipyard property across the Norfolk and Western Railroad tracks at what is now the East Yard. Eventually the bell made its way across the tracks and was mounted on a tall pole in front of the colonial

This circa 1925 photo shows a group of shipyard workers in front of the old colonial farmhouse. Carl Colonna Sr. is the man to the left in a suit and tie. The tall pole with the shipyard bell can be seen in front of the house. The old house served as an early office for the shipyard.

farmhouse that served as the residence of Charles J. Colonna and family and also as the shipyard office. At that time it was used to signal the beginning of each workday, lunchtime, and completion of the workday. The paymaster also rang it on paydays. The bell after having been professionally cleaned was permanently mounted in March 2009, on the post in the lobby of the new office building, and is now rung each time the shipyard is awarded a contract amounting to $5 million or more. Con-

The old shipyard bell, after having been professionally cleaned and mounted on a new pole, now stands in the lobby of the shipyard office building.

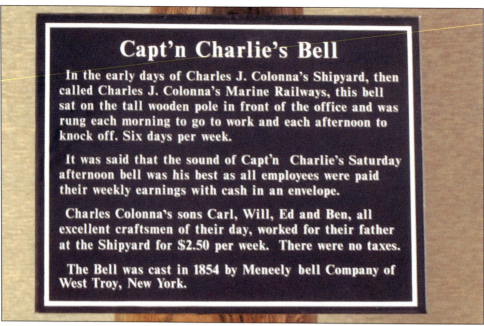

This plaque, which is mounted on the pole below the shipyard bell, identifies it as "Capt'n Charlie's Bell."

In February 2011, Richard Sobocinski stands nearby as Anna Nowland prepares to ring the bell. The bell is rung each time the shipyard is awarded a contract amounting to at least $5 million.

tract awards from $1 million but less than $5 million are celebrated by the ringing of smaller bells in the individual offices.

West Yard

Development of the West Yard was almost like designing and constructing a completely new shipbuilding and repair facility. Although it is intended to be a part of the Main Yard the distance between the resources of the existing yard and the new development is considerable. However, at the time of this writing (2011) it is expected that the West Yard will also use the management and large shop

The initial testing of the Marine Travelift took place on a cold windy afternoon in April 2010. After testing, the first customer lift was the tug Roanoke, *which is owned by the Vane Brothers. This lift took place on April 21, 2010.*

support from the Main Yard. The complete development of the West Yard, which is scheduled to be accomplished in phases, will represent a significant investment and is expected to require several years. The property involved in this development was purchased by Colonna's in December 1948, and had been underutilized for a very long time.

On Friday, February 27, 2009, Thomas Godfrey Jr., company president and chief executive officer (CEO), announced that the company was planning phase one of a $20-million expansion. At that time, plans had been submitted to the Army Corps of Engineers for the project. Work, which included the dredging of 69,450 cubic yards from the river just west of Pescara Creek, and construction of a 550-foot bulkhead, a 238-foot pier, and a 328-foot pier along the Eastern Branch of the Elizabeth River, was begun in the second half of 2009. Those improvements were necessary to accommodate the 1,000-metric-ton Marine Travelift that was placed in operation in 2010. By early December 2009, the first parts of the travelift arrived and by the week of the fourteenth assembly began taking place.

This 2011 Polaris Ranger 4x4, which tows a fifteen-passenger tram, now provides convenient transportation to and from the West Yard.

The travelift has a lifting capacity of 1,000 metric tons, an inside clearance width of 62 feet, a maximum block spacing of 91 feet, and a draft capacity of 27 feet. Its overall height is 66 feet. The tires alone are 12.5 feet in height. This massive piece of equipment is the largest of its kind in the world and costs in the neighborhood of $7 million. The questions that may arise are: How is it operated?, What is it supposed to do?, and How does it help the overall operation of the shipyard? To begin with a person with a remote control unit guides the travelift onto the two piers where its slings are lowered into the water. A vessel such as a yacht, tugboat, or barge is then floated between the two piers after which the travelift carefully lifts the vessel out of the water and carries it to a designated place where scheduled maintenance or repairs will be accomplished. This development of the West Yard and acquisition of the travelift allows the floating dry docks and marine railways at the Main Yard to be dedicated to larger vessels.

By July 21, 2009, work had begun on phase one of the expansion of the West Yard. Heavy equipment and pilings had been delivered to the site and some leveling of the land was underway. Work on the new bulkhead was begun later in the week. By late November there was a lot of activity in the yard, dredging was taking place, and work on the piers and bulkheads was well underway.

It was on Wednesday, April 14, 2010, a cold windy day, that many workers and spectators gathered in the afternoon to witness the initial test of the Marine Travelift. The travelift was guided onto the two piers and its slings were lowered into the water. After that, a test barge was maneuvered into the slip between the piers and various tests were performed by filling the barge with varying amounts of water. The testing met all requirements. After that, the first customer lift was the tug *Roanoke*, owned by the Vane Brothers. It was lifted from the waters of the Elizabeth River and taken to its designated work area.

By early June 2010, phase one was complete. This part of the development included dredging, a new bulkhead, two new piers, installation of utilities, the Marine Travelift, and ground preparation for use by the travelift.

In December 2010, Colonna's Shipyard acquired an additional 7.4 acres from K-Sea Norfolk, a transportation corporation that deals in tugboats and barges. The property that faces South Main Street in Berkley adjoins the existing property of the West Yard and should increase its capacity from ten to fifteen docking berths. An existing two-story office building on this property will be used for offices to support work in the West Yard, and also the Colonna Down River division. In addition to the two-story office building this property also contained several large storage tanks, which were removed in early October 2011. This recently acquired property fits in well with plans for phase two enlargement of the West Yard, which includes additional ship berths, office space, and a pier.

Phases two and three of the expansion will eventually follow phase one and their enlargement of the West Yard could possibly result in an increase of about 10 or 15 percent to the existing work force.

As mentioned above, the distance between the West Yard and the Main Yard is considerable. To help reduce the travel time between the two a new vehicle, a tram has been added. The new vehicle is a Polaris Ranger 4x4 that tows a fifteen-passenger tram. Several golf carts, bicycles, and a shuttle are also available as transportation between the yards.

In October 2010, after receiving a new paint job the Staten Island Ferry/Spirit of America *was made ready for the long tow back home.*

New York Ferries

Throughout the years it has not been unusual to see a New York ferry receiving maintenance at Colonna's Shipyard. When first seeing a ferry from New York in the yard I asked why come so far for maintenance and repairs? The answer was "it is less expensive and the quality of work is great." In 2009, Colonna's was awarded a five-year $71.5-million contract to service six of the eight Staten Island ferries on a rotating schedule. Each of the six ferries is expected to visit the shipyard at least twice during the five-year period. Three ferries a year will make the thirty-six-hour trip from New York to Norfolk. After completion of the work, the ferry is "buttoned-up," inspected by the Coast Guard, and is towed back home, which takes another thirty-six hours.

In April 2009 the *Andrew J. Barberi* was towed from New York to Norfolk. After receiving routine maintenance and repairs it headed back to New York on Thursday, June 11, 2009. The *Barberi*, which entered service in 1981 is capable

These five men, left to right: Bob Cotes, Chris Hartwig, Kenny Mebane, Lacy Vess, and Kelly Boykin, oversaw construction of the barge Margaret.

of carrying six thousand passengers and has a crew of fifteen plus one attendant. The boat is 310 feet long, 69 feet 10 inches wide, has a draft of 13 feet 6 inches, weighs 3,335 gross tons, and its seven-thousand-horsepower engine produces a service speed of sixteen knots. In September 2011, the *Barberi* made a second trip to Colonna's Shipyard.

Federal Stimulus Funding

In August 2009, the US Maritime Administration announced that five local shipyards would receive a total of more than $7.8 million in federal stimulus funding as part of a program to assist small shipyards. Colonna's Shipyard received $1.96 million and planned to use it for a wastewater treatment barge. Vice President/Contracts Richard "Soby" Sobocinski stated that it was an environmental

This building served as the main office of the shipyard for many years until the new three-story building was completed. It still serves as the office for Steel America and possibly others.

issue and the barge was needed to protect that area of the Elizabeth River near the shipyard.

Barge *Margaret*

On Wednesday morning, March 23, 2011, the barge *Margaret*, which was named for the wife of the shipyard founder Charles J. Colonna, was christened by Evelyn Colonna, wife of Bill Colonna, grandson of Charles and Margaret Colonna. The ceremony, which took place at the Main Yard, was attended by a large group of shipyard employees.

On Wednesday morning, March 23, 2011, the barge Margaret, named for the wife of Charles J. Colonna, was christened by Evelyn Colonna, wife of Bill Colonna, grandson of Charles and Margaret Colonna.

Regina Wallace, security guard, checks a customer as he leaves the shipyard.

Captain Ballard, head security guard, is shown standing duty at the entrance to the Main Yard.

Charles J. Colonna—Sculptures

In February 2011, W. W. Colonna Jr. commissioned David Turner of Turner Sculptures, based on the Eastern Shore of Virginia, to produce two bronze busts of his grandfather, shipyard founder Charles J. Colonna. On April 14, 2011, Mr. Turner delivered the sculptures to the shipyard where he placed one on a pedestal in the lobby of the main office building and the other in the boardroom on the third floor where Charles J. will be able to oversee all future meetings of the Board of Directors.

This sculpture of Charles Jones Colonna, founder of Colonna's Shipyard, was mounted in the lobby of the shipyard office building on April 14, 2011. A similar one was also placed in the boardroom on the third floor.

Three members of Colonna's younger generation are, from left to right, Karen Colonna, W. W. Colonna III, and Randall Crutchfield. This picture was taken in the boardroom in November 2011. The sculpture of Charles J. Colonna, the founder of the shipyard can be seen between Karen and her brother W. W. Colonna III. The paintings behind them are, from left to right, Captain Will Colonna and Captain Ben Colonna.

2000–2011

This photo of the shipyard was taken on November 20, 2010. The East Yard is that small area to the right and across the railroad tracks. The Main Yard is in the center of this aerial view and the West Yard is to the left of Pescara Creek and at the top left. The West Yard now extends to South Main Street in the Berkley section of the city of Norfolk.

127

Chapter VII

Colonna's People

While much has been written about a select few of Colonna's early people, mostly members of the family, which contributed to the formative years of the shipyard, there are many others that need to be recognized for helping to make it what it is today. It was my pleasure to interview a cross section of more recent employees as well as several members of the Board of Directors; in doing so I found them to be not only very knowledgeable, but also very dedicated to the success of the corporation.

Early Employees

Bob Nichols—Longest Serving Employee

Many early employees spent a large part of their lives working at Colonna's Shipyard. According to available records, Bob Nichols, a wood caulker, who was hired around 1903 by the founder, Charles J. Colonna, was employed at Colonna's for sixty-eight years. Other than members of the family that were born in the colonial farmhouse on shipyard property and spent most of their lives working at Colonna's, Bob holds the record for years of employment at the yard. Captains Carl, Ben, and Will Colonna were young men when he hired on. Bob worked for the Colonna's so long that he became like a member of the family and in his old age reported to work when his health allowed; however, the Colonna family saw to it that he remained on the payroll. In his later years, Bob resided in a house on nearby Indian River Road.

Working sixty-eight years at one place is really hard to believe; however, the story does not end there. Bob Nichols was employed at a sawmill in Berkley for eighteen years before joining Colonna's Shipyard and even before that at the ripe old age of five he began working at the mill helping his father shovel sawdust. Doing the math we see that Bob's working life covered more than eighty-six years and he lived to be almost one hundred years of age.

Bob Nichols worked sixty-eight years at Colonna's Shipyard. Nichols was hired as a wood caulker by the founder Charles J. Colonna. At the time of this writing, he holds the record for the most years in the employ of the shipyard. This picture was taken in June 1953.

Joseph Timothy Wilder (Joe)

Mr. Wilder was christened J. T. Wilder and was later given the name Joseph Timothy Wilder. With the first name Joseph it wasn't long before he acquired the nickname "Joe."

Charles J. Colonna hired Joe as a ship carpenter in the latter 1800s. He eventually became foreman of the carpenters. On August 5, 1929, Joe was stricken with a heart attack and died on a workbench in the carpenter shop.

Henry Cleveland Wilder Sr. (Cleve)

Cleve Wilder, son of Joseph Timothy Wilder, like his father, was a ship carpenter and an early employee of Colonna's Shipyard. Cleve became employed at the yard on June 21, 1907, and also like his father, eventually became foreman of the carpenters. On four different occasions when work became slack, Cleve was forced to leave; however, all together he was employed at Colonna's Shipyard for fifty-three years.

Left to right: Benjamin O. Colonna and Henry Cleveland (Cleve) Wilder. Cleve, an early employee, was hired June 21, 1907, and eventually became foreman of the carpenters. On August 6, 1918, Cleve was working on the underside of a barge when a support gave way and his right arm was crushed to the point where it had to be amputated. He worked at Colonna's Shipyard a total of fifty-three years. This photo was taken in 1916.

Sometimes shipyard work can be dangerous and accidents do occasionally happen. On August 6, 1918, Cleve Wilder was hammering on the underside of a barge when a support gave way and his right arm was crushed to the point that it had to be amputated. However, two months later he was back on the job.

Hugo Bernagozzi—Superintendent of Foreign Trade

When he was just fifteen years of age, Hugo Bernagozzi left his home in Bologna, Italy, and came to the United States. He initially made New York City his place of residence, but in the early1900s, came to the Norfolk area, where he applied for employment at Colonna's Shipyard. Captains Will and Ben Colonna, who were president and vice president respectively of the shipyard, hired him. Hugo proved to be an ambitious and well-liked employee. He liked to joke and so the other employees did not take him seriously when he bragged about being friends with Charles "Lucky" Luciano, the Italian mobster who became the father of organized crime in the United States and Giovanni Martinelli, an Italian operatic tenor.

One day a highly polished black car drove into the shipyard and parked. One of its occupants got out, went into the office and asked to see Hugo Bernagozzi. The receptionist directed him to Hugo's office. The man spent a considerable amount of time visiting with Hugo. As he was leaving, the two embraced and the visitor told Hugo, "If you ever need anything you know you can always count on Lucky." One of the shipyard workers saw the car and noticed that a man standing next to it seemed to be acting as a guard and when he opened the door for the visitor to get in he saw there were at least two men sitting in the back seat and there was a Tommy gun on the front seat. After the men left he reported what he had seen to Captains Will and Ben. They then went to Hugo's office and asked him whom his visitor was. Hugo hesitated for a few seconds and finally told them that it was his friend Lucky. One of them then asked, "Lucky who." Finally Hugo admitted that his visitor had been Lucky Luciano.

In addition to having boasted about being friends with Giovanni Martinelli Bernagozzi often spoke about having sung with Enrico Caruso another famous Italian tenor. And of course no one believed him; that is, until one evening when he and some of his fellow workers were attending a party and one person began playing the piano and another the violin. Out of the sound of the music, suddenly there was heard the most wonderful singing voice and yes it was Hugo. So, who knows, maybe he did sing with Caruso and yes he was definitely friends with Lucky Luciano and Giovanni Martinelli, for they both were known to have visited him at the shipyard. However, after a successful career at Colonna's Shipyard, Hugo retired and spent the rest of his years living in Norfolk.

Thomas Walter Godfrey, Jr.—President and Chief Executive Officer (CEO)

Thomas Walter Godfrey Jr.

Before joining Colonna's Shipyard, Inc., Thomas Walter Godfrey Jr. received his BA degree in management economics from Hampden-Sydney College in 1978. After graduation, he served as management supervisor with E. R. Carpenter, Inc., of Richmond, Virginia, until 1979 when he became ship superintendent and estimator at Allied Marine Industries, Inc., of Norfolk, Virginia. In 1983, Godfrey joined Colonna's Shipyard as estimator and contracts manager. The year 1986 proved to be an important one for Mr. Godfrey in that he not only became director of finance at Colonna's Shipyard, he also received his MBA degree from the University of Richmond. In 1992, he became director of operations, a position that he held until 1993 when he became president/CEO of Colonna's Shipyard.

Thomas Godfrey worked hard and his contributions to Colonna's were many. He cut overhead costs, improved day-to-day operations and among other things, helped see the shipyard through the burdens brought on by bankruptcy.

In a letter written May 21, 1999, Mr. Godfrey announced his resignation and stated that he would be moving to Houston, Texas, to assume the position of vice president of ship repair with First Wave/New Park Shipbuilding. In the same letter he stated that Ray Burkart would fill the position of president at Colonna's Shipyard, effective May 24, 1999. The move to Texas proved to be unsuccessful and by early 2000 he was back in Virginia and in his former position as president/CEO at Colonna's Shipyard.

In an open memo, dated February 23, 2000, to all the employees of Colonna's Shipyard, Godfrey thanked everyone for the warm welcome that he received on his return and especially thanked Bill Colonna for allowing him the privilege of leading the corporation into a great future.

At the time of this writing Thomas W. Godfrey continues in the position of president/CEO of Colonna's Shipyard. During his tenure the shipyard has grown rapidly in both facility and manpower.

Carl M. Albero—Vice Chairman of the Board of Directors

Carl M. Albero holds a bachelor's degree in chemical engineering and master's degrees in mechanical engineering and business administration. He retired from the US Navy as a captain and among his many tours of duty, served as engineering officer on the aircraft carrier USS *John F. Kennedy*.

After retirement from the Navy he began what proved to be a successful second career in engineering services and consulting. He later founded several contracting firms and eventually one of them became the largest provider of engineering services to the United States fleet of aircraft carriers.

In the year 2004, on the advice of Dick Hopkins, a member of the Board of Directors, Chairman W. W. Colonna Jr. contacted Mr. Albero and asked him if he would serve on the Board of Colonna's Shipyard. He agreed and is now approaching his tenth year using his talents and contacts for the betterment of the Colonna team. In his years on the Board he has been instrumental in hiring well-qualified people and placing them in key positions. Mr. Albero may be described as a mentor, advisor, and visionary. It is through his efforts that Colonna's now has a special division that seeks out and manages government work.

Waverley Berkley III—Secretary and Corporate Counsel

Waverley Berkley III graduated from Maury High School in Norfolk, Virginia. He subsequently attended the University of Virginia, graduating in 1952, and three years later completed law school also at the University of Virginia. At that time he was sworn into the US Marine Corps as a second lieutenant. After three years of active duty he transferred to inactive status and served in that capacity for six years. In 1964, after nine years of service and obtaining the rank of captain, he resigned from the Marine Corps.

A History of Colonna's Shipyard and Its People

After his active military service, Waverley returned to Norfolk and became involved in the practice of admiralty law. In 1977, he became an attorney for Colonna's Shipyard and has served the corporation ever since. Today he is a member of the Board of Directors and serves as secretary and corporate attorney.

Willoughby Warren Colonna III (Billy)

W. W. Colonna III began working in the family shipyard when he was but nine years of age. In the early 1960s he worked in the electric shop where he picked up nuts and bolts that were covered with paint. It was his job to clean them. This meant removing the paint all the way down to the metal. The first week he worked about sixty hours, drew his pay in cash and then quit. However, it wasn't long before he resumed work at the yard.

As a youngster, he also rode around the yard with the truck drivers and kept company with the crane operators when they were working. His high school years were spent at Hargrave Military Academy in Chatham, Virginia. During summer breaks he always kept busy by working at the shipyard.

In 1973, Bill became a full-time employee and remained in the business until 2005 when at age fifty he took an early retirement. Some of his fondest memories were the days that he worked for his grandfather, W. W. Colonna Sr. Starting in 1973; he began a rotation of all the shops in the yard, which included five years in the plate shop where he learned to fabricate parts of all sizes and shapes. During this time he became a certified welder and a certified diver.

Prior to 1986, the officers and directors of Colonna's Shipyard began searching for a floating dry dock. It became Bill's job to find one. This project not only included trips throughout the United States but also trips to Europe and the Mediterranean. He eventually found one in Amsterdam, Holland.

W. W. Colonna III has served the family shipyard in many ways and at one time even served as vice president. He no longer works for Colonna's Shipyard, but is serving as president of Norfolk Barge Company.

Karen Colonna—Director of Risk Management

After graduating from First Colonial High School in Virginia Beach, Karen decided that she would like to work in the family shipyard. She had office experience but her interest led her to work in the outside machine shop. A combination of being the owner's novice daughter and a shop full of overly protective machinists made for a very short, but enlightening work experience. Her stint in the outside machine shop gave Karen a deep appreciation for the skill and character of shipyard trades people, an appreciation that continues with her to this day.

After her experience in the outside machine shop, Karen went to work for Health Food Centers, Inc., a business that was established in 1960 by W. W. Colonna Jr. This move proved to be very successful, for Karen worked her way up from salesclerk to general manager of seven locations. Her next move after leaving Health Food Centers was marriage and raising her two sons, Quinn Colonna Duckett and Heath Colonna Duckett.

In 1988 she received her degree in business administration from Old Dominion University and over the next few years she worked for several companies.

It was in 2005, when her brother W. W. Colonna III took an early retirement from the shipyard that she received a call from her father asking her if she would consider coming back to work at the shipyard. After giving it some thought, she told him that she would work for three months without pay before making a commitment. After three months Karen accepted a full-time position as project manager and Webmaster.

In January 2009, three US Navy ships were at Colonna's Shipyard for repairs. One of them was the USS *Freedom* (LCS 1) the US Navy's first littoral combat ship, which possessed amazing capabilities. Karen, as facility security officer, was placed in charge of access to the shipyard. The *Freedom* was visited by over four thousand visitors, which included twenty-eight flag officers, numerous foreign dignitaries, distinguished guests, and contractors. For her service Karen received a letter of commendation from Rear Admiral J. A. Murdoch.

Today, Karen is director of risk management for the shipyard and has the honor of being the first woman member of Colonna's Board of Directors. Recently, her father began turning over the ownership and responsibility of the shipyard to members of the younger generations.

Randall A. Crutchfield—Production Superintendent

Randall A. Crutchfield graduated from Norfolk Academy in 2005 and received a bachelor's degree with a major in international business from the University of North Carolina, Chapel Hill, in 2009. He plans to eventually return to school and receive a master's degree in business administration.

Since becoming employed at Colonna's Shipyard, he has served in several phases of the operation to include assistant facilities director where he was involved in the expansion of the West Yard. In this position he was a member of a team that traveled to Wisconsin where they were able to witness part of the construction of the Marine Travelift that was being built for Colonna's Shipyard.

For eight or nine months he was assigned to Down River, a division of Colonna's Shipyard. Down River is made up of a workforce or field team that travels to other locations and performs work that otherwise may not be able to be accomplished at the Main Yard.

Crutchfield now serves as a production superintendent in the main shipyard where he may be assigned to one or more vessels. From the very beginning until the day of completion he is responsible for every phase of repair or modification made to those vessels.

Recently, Randall A. Crutchfield was appointed to the Board of Directors of Colonna's Shipyard.

David L. Dipersio—Vice President/Chief Financial Officer

David L. Dipersio, received degrees from Thomas Nelson University and the College of William and Mary. He became an employee at Colonna's Shipyard in July 2002. In addition to being chief financial officer he is also in charge of personnel in the Accounting, Human Resources, and Information Technology Departments. Approximately thirty people work for Dipersio.

Most of the shipyard employees will say that he is the most important person in the yard because he is the man that manages the money and see that all the workers are paid and on time. It is also his job to make sure that all suppliers are paid as well.

David is also the main man when it comes to audits and they can cause a person to have some real bad headaches if the figures don't balance like they should. The job can be summed up in these few words, "Money in and Money Out."

Mark Essert—Director of Facilities

Mark Essert began his shipyard career in the Docking Department of Colonna's Shipyard in 1985. That job involved mostly hauling, moving, and placement of vessels. In 1992, he became dock master and remained in that position until 2005.

In 2006, he was promoted to director of facilities, a position that he still holds in the year 2011. As director of facilities, Mark is in charge of maintenance, new construction, and certification of a variety of equipment.

J. Douglas Forrest—Former Vice President of Colonna's Shipyard

Doug Forrest is originally from the Bronx, a borough of New York City. When asked about his educational background, he replied, "I have none." At the age of fifteen he began working on small boats in the New York harbor. Upon reaching the age of seventeen he enlisted in the US Coast Guard and served two years as a boatswain (bo's'n). After his tour of duty in the Coast Guard his maritime career led him to passenger and freight vessels in the United States and the West Indies. One of the vessels that he later worked on was the container ship *Argonaut*, which was constructed at Bath Iron Works in 1979 for the Farrell Lines. The *Argonaut* was named for a clipper ship that was built in the 1800s.

Ultimately Forrest was named port captain of New York Harbor, became responsible for chemical tankers, and eventually gravitated to ship repair. He later became vice president of Arthur Tickle Engineering Works. It was from Tickle that many hospitals, large department stores, and other industries purchased steam for their operation. In addition to furnishing steam, Tickle also worked on commercial equipment.

Just prior to 1990 some of the officials at Colonna's Shipyard had begun to push aside steady work such as that offered by tugs, fishing boats, and other commercial vessels and started depending on work from predator customers such as the US government. Sometimes the government is not too dependable especially when politics enters the picture. This is what happened prior to 1990 and forced Colonna's into bankruptcy. Colonna's Shipyard was well known and had a good reputation throughout the maritime industry. They were known for being dependable and producing high quality work.

Mr. Forrest arrived in Norfolk during the summer of 1991and became vice president of Colonna's Shipyard, a position that he held until the year 2000. Near the end of 1991, Colonna's workload began to steadily increase.

In 2000, Forrest retired at the age of fifty. Today (2011) he is president of Paradise Point Marine, Inc., with offices on Plume Street in downtown Norfolk, Virginia.

Nevin E. Hedrick Jr. (Turk)—Manager of Commercial Contracts

Nevin E. Hedrick became employed at Colonna's Shipyard on June 1, 1973. As his title indicates, he submits bids on commercial work for the shipyard. In order to bid on commercial work, he has to look closely at each job, determine what materials will be needed, the cost of those materials, and the amount and types of labor involved. In figuring the labor he must take into account the hourly wage of the various trades. The cost of overhead, as well as a certain percentage of profit must also be included in each bid. We might say that he does a lot of planning and estimating for the corporation.

Once the contract has been signed and work begins another part of his job is to keep track of the cost and make sure the work remains on schedule. This information is reported at the weekly sales meeting.

Most of the commercial work is repeat business. It differs from that of government work in that commercial work involves working more with people and personalities while dealing with the government more paper work is involved.

W. Vance Hull—Director of Yacht Services

W. Vance Hull graduated from Maury High School in Norfolk in 1976 and received his degree in economics from Hampden-Sydney College in 1980. Vance began his employment as director of yacht services at Colonna's in August 1999. His first job was to oversee repairs to the yacht *Monitor*, which was in the yard when he arrived. One of the requirements of his position is to search out and bring yacht business to the shipyard. In order to accomplish this requirement he has traveled extensively in both the United States and Europe.

The repair and modification of yachts is an industry that puts many people to work. While the initial cost of a yacht may be in the millions of dollars the upkeep, operation and in some cases modifications, can also run into millions of dollars. It is quite obvious that yacht ownership is for the wealthier among us.

When the economy turns sour so does the amount of available yacht repair work, for the owners will become more cautious with their money and will spend only what is absolutely necessary.

On April 11, 2010, the M/Y (Motor Yacht) *Aquarius* became a part of Colonna history by being the first vessel of any kind to berth at the new West Yard facility. After pier side repairs were accomplished The *Aquarius* resumed its mission as a floating hotel for the owner and his guest.

Following the *Aquarius* project the M/Y *Kiss the Sky*, which is Russian owned, made an emergency stop at Colonna's. After repairs it continued its voyage to New York. Before leaving a tentative agreement was made that the yacht would return in November 2010 for its scheduled maintenance and check of some engineering items.

Charles (Charlie) R. Jones—Motorman

Charlie Jones' life in the workforce has been one of real interest. His earlier years were spent working as a barber in the Southgate Plaza Shopping Center in South Norfolk, after which he worked for Capital Foods in Norfolk. When Capital Foods went out of business in 1967, Jones went to the state employment office to see if there were any jobs available. Fortunately, Colonna's Shipyard needed a few good men and Charlie was hired in March 1967, as a third-class helper in the paint shop at $1.54 per hour. After approximately six months in the paint shop he was transferred to the electric shop where he learned the electrician trade and later was involved in shipboard installation of radar systems. He eventually worked his way up to leading man in the electric shop. Throughout the years Charlie became interested in and learned other trades in the yard, one of them being that of motorman.

At that time the marine railways were operated by "Tato" Beasily. When Beasily died Captain Ben Colonna, president of the shipyard, wanted Charlie to assume the position of motorman. The head of the electric shop did not want him to go, however, Captain Ben had his way and Charlie became operator of the marine railways.

During his forty-four years at Colonna's Shipyard, Charlie Jones has held several different positions, including a stint as assistant superintendent. At this time (2011), his job is that of motorman and his duties include operation of the marine railways, air compressors, and burning systems.

Kenneth Mebane—Vice President of Steel America

Kenneth Mebane began his employment at Colonna's Shipyard on April 19, 1978, and worked in the pipe shop until 1980. Soon afterwards he was transferred to facilities and maintenance, and was engaged in the overhaul and upgrade of No. 3 marine railway. In 1985, after thirty days of dredging, he was involved in the construction of pier No. 6, which was built in order to accommodate Navy vessels. The next year would see the arrival of the eighteen-thousand-metric-ton floating dry dock and upgrade to some of the existing shops. In 1996, as a member of what was known then as the "Colonna Industrial Group," he and others went out seeking work for the machine shop. Between 1996 and 1997, 3 million pounds of steel were used in fabrication work for the Ford Motor Company. In the year 2000, Kenneth working along with Bill Colonna, founded Steel America.

In February 2009, Steel America became certified by the US Navy as an approved propulsion-shaft-repair facility. In April 2009, a newly acquired lathe, which would be of help in servicing larger propulsion shafts, arrived at the inside machine shop.

Steel America's workload, both commercial and government, continues to increase. In the year 2010 Steel America was busy constructing sector gates and new caissons for the Norfolk Naval Shipyard.

Also in 2010, Steel America's workforce consisted of 107 full-time employees plus eight apprentices. Mebane devotes a fair amount of his time to working with and teaching these apprentices individually and also as a group.

In April 2010, Mr. Mebane celebrated thirty-two years of devoted service to Colonna's Shipyard. During that time he made a special effort to learn not only his position, but often the position of other employees as well. During those years he has been known to spend many extra hours at the yard and at times those hours included Christmas Eve and even a part of Christmas Day. Now that is real devotion to the job.

RADM(ret.) Mike Nowakowski—Vice President/ Defense Contracting Group

As a retired admiral with thirty-three years of service to the US Navy, Mr. Nowakowski brings a considerable amount of experience to the Colonna team. His knowledge of federal contracts and connections in dealing with government officials has made him and will continue to make him a valuable employee.

In addition to managing existing contracts and continuously looking for new work, Mike oversees Down River, which is a division of Colonna's Shipyard. Down River has a reputation of being ready to travel anywhere, at any time to accomplish

Cassion No. 8 for the Norfolk Naval Shipyard was built in 2011 by Steel America, a division of Colonna's Shipyard.

ship repair and maintenance. Their previous projects have covered not only the Hampton Roads area, but also all of the East Coast and foreign ports as well

Richard Sobocinski (Soby)—Vice President/Contracts

Richard Sobocinski received his bachelor's degree in mechanical engineering from Northeastern University in Boston, Massachusetts, in 1973 and his master's of business administration from Babson College in Wellesley, Massachusetts, in 1979. From 1969 until 1983, he was employed at Bethlehem Steel Corporation and from 1983 until 2002 he worked at Bath Iron Works Corporation, which later became General Dynamics.

In 2002, Soby joined Colonna's Shipyard, where he became engaged in both commercial and military contracts and to a certain degree, foreign sales. He is also involved in planning and estimating and management of various programs. He has played a major part in the growth of the corporation sales, which during the past five years have almost tripled.

W. W. Colonna Jr., owner of the shipyard, credits Sobocinski with bringing the one-thousand-metric-ton Marine Travelift to Colonna's. When asked about his involvement, Soby says, he just attended a boat show where he saw a much smaller version, inquired about the possibility of building a larger one and the rest is history. The travelift at Colonna's, which was put into service in April 2010, is the largest in the world and has already proven its worth. It has made waiting to get access to a dry dock a thing of the past for many of the yard's customers.

Sandra Spriggs—Storeroom Attendant

Sandra Spriggs hired on at Colonna's Shipyard on March 27, 1978. Her career path began as a timekeeper helper in the machine shop where she acquired an interest and knowledge in the several trades affiliated with the machine shop. Later, she also gained the knowledge needed for the position of storeroom attendant and when that person retired she was able to fill the vacancy.

Her duties as storeroom attendant are many. Ms. Spriggs supplies material for all the jobs in the shipyard as well as those used by its divisions. She keeps track of inventory and restocks materials and parts as needed. There are times when replacement parts are made by different manufacturers, using the same specifications, but for some reason the part built by one manufacturer works better than the others. When that occurs, Ms. Spriggs recommends that the Purchasing Department order from the manufacturer that makes the better part.

Charlie Sutton—Director of Down River, A Division of Colonna's Shipyard

Charlie Sutton, a native of Virginia Beach and graduate of Bayside schools, has been in the shipyard business since 1975. His career in the industry began at Newport News Shipbuilding where he spent about five years working on new construction of submarines. After that he went to work for Allied Towing and then around 1983/84 he became employed at Colonna's Shipyard.

After about fifteen years of sticking to repairs of commercial vessels, Colonna's decided in January 1984, to resume bidding on government work. On May 15, 1984, the minesweeper *Fortify* came into the yard. During his employment at Colonna's Shipyard, Charlie worked on the USS *Fortify* and other government vessels.

When Superior Marine, a new company, entered the shipyard industry, Charlie left Colonna's and went with them as vice president. He later left Superior and hired on at Earl Industries where he became senior program manager and worked for about twenty years.

In January 2011, he was contacted by Tom Godfrey, president and CEO of Colonna's Shipyard and was offered the position of director of Down River. He accepted and returned to Colonna's in late January 2011.

Stephen Walker—Vice President/Operations

Stephen Walker is originally from Monmouth, Maine, and received his BS degree in marine engineering from Maine Maritime Academy. After college he became employed at Bethlehem Steel where he underwent a two-year management-training program. Walker later went to Boston, Massachusetts, where he was hired by General Ship and Engineering Works. When the ship-repair business in Boston began to decline Stephen went to work for Avondale Industries in New Orleans, Louisiana. During his fifteen years there he was involved in the construction of fleet oilers, LSDs, and other vessels. He was also engaged in large ship-repair projects. Mr. Walker is the holder of Coast Guard engineering licenses in both steam and diesel with unlimited horsepower.

Pictured here is Colonna's Shipyard Vice President of Operations Stephen Walker.

The Logistics Support Vessel (LSV4) Lt. Gen. William B. Bunker *returned to the Army watercraft fleet at Fort Eustis, Virginia, in November 2011 after the successful completion of its six-month On Condition Cyclic Maintenance and three-month Service Life Extension Program (SLEP), performed at Colonna's Shipyard.*

So what brought Stephen Walker to Colonna's Shipyard? After all he had been used to working at large facilities and Colonna's was a much smaller operation. He knew the yard had undergone some hard times and to make the move in employment was very risky. He felt that maybe he could be of help. He attributes this move to that fact and he also liked the way W. W. Colonna Jr. and Thomas W. Godfrey Jr. did business. They were both good men and didn't mind taking a gamble if it meant improving the operation of Colonna's Shipyard. With all this in mind, Walker joined the Colonna team on April 8, 2002, and it has been full steam ahead ever since. When he leaves home about 4:30 in the morning he has no idea when he will return, for he will put in as many hours as are needed to get the job done.

His position requires that he handle facilities, maintenance, material purchasing, production, and other duties as needed. At this time the yard handles about

230 dry dockings per year and that does not include the West Yard. A lot of the work involves structural and mechanical repairs. One of the yard's contracts is the repair and maintenance of the Staten Island Ferries. Another program that Walker is concerned with is the Ship Life Extension Program of the US Army LSVs (Logistics Support Vehicle), which are vessels that are less than three hundred feet in length. Although each is assigned a number each is also named for a person of importance. This program adds approximately fifteen years to the life expectancy of each vessel.

A strong commitment to commercial work such as tugboats, barges, fishing vessels, etc., exists at the yard, but Walker said, "A real effort is made to keep a 50/50 balance between commercial and government work. The idea behind this is when one market is down, the other market picks up."

Frank Wheatley—Compliance Director

Frank Wheatley began his employment at Colonna's Shipyard on March 29, 1984, as a marine electrician. He had attended a vocational school where he learned his trade. Before coming to Colonna's he was employed by Allied Repair Services for a period of five years.

Frank is originally from Delaware, but since his father was in the Navy and stationed at Norfolk, the family relocated to the area. His father was an electronic technician and in order to make additional money, he took a job moonlighting on ships that were docked at Colonna's Shipyard. Not only did Frank's father have a connection with Colonna's, but his grandfather did as well. His grandfather owned a barge that he used to haul coal. In addition to the barge providing a means for making a living, it also served as a place for the family to live. The family consisted of his grandfather, his grandmother, and two aunts. The barge was often tied up at Colonna's Shipyard. On one occasion when the barge was tied up at Colonna's his grandfather went over to Berkley to attend to a matter of importance and while he was gone a storm came up and blew the barge out in the middle of the Elizabeth River. Of course the barge was retrieved and all was well.

So what does a "Compliance Director" do? His duties are many. To begin with he is an environmentalist and as such he has to deal with organizations such as the Occupational Safety and Health Administration (OSHA) that inspects the facility for compliance with its regulations. He is also head of the "Safety Department and Security." So when you pass through the gate at the entranced to the shipyard those folks in the brown uniforms work for Mr. Wheatley.

Sherry Wheatley—Accounting Manager

Sherry began working as a temporary employee at Colonna's Shipyard in August 1987. However, she soon became a permanent member of the shipyard family and worked as a timekeeper helper. In that position she kept account of the hours worked by some of the employees. This also included keeping a record of hours charged against specific job numbers.

In her present position as "accounting manager" she oversees day-to-day operations in the Accounting Department, which includes accounting procedures, accounts (moneys received, the amount kept and the amount spent), payment of taxes and payroll. Another important and time-consuming part of her job is the participation in various types of audits.

Ardell S. Wright—Tool Room Attendant

Ardell began her employment at Colonna's Shipyard on March 18, 1978. She described the tool room at that time as being a small red building. Many things have changed in the more than thirty-three years that she has been issuing tools to the workers. In 1978, when a worker needed a tool or tools a written record was kept on paper, then later the workers used chips the size of a quarter when drawing tools from the tool room, and today all record of tool issues are kept on computer.

Ms. Wright's position requires that she possess knowledge of the many different trades and tools used in the shipyard. When asked if she liked her job, her response was a smile along with a resounding yes and a comment that "the people are among the best." As an added comment she mentioned that in her early employment the shipyard had only one truck, but now there is a fleet consisting of many trucks.

Happy Employees

Every employee that I had the pleasure of interviewing for this history of Colonna's Shipyard spoke very highly of their fellow employees and the corporation supervision. Some even said that the niceness begins at the top and filters down to all the others.

Chapter VIII
Employee Activities and Benefits

Several times a year in acknowledgement for a job well done and out of respect for the welfare of its employees, the management of Colonna's Shipyard presents the workers with various gifts or rewards; such as a free picnic-type lunch, which is usually held about twice a year when the weather is pleasant. Then around July a large truck filled with watermelons arrives from North Carolina and each worker receives a big ripe watermelon filled with sweetness. In November, just in time for each employee's Thanksgiving dinner table another large truck arrives; this one is filled with turkeys, each weighing about twelve pounds. And in December an annual Christmas party is held for the workers. As winter approaches each

About once or twice a year when the weather is nice the employees of Colonna's Shipyard are treated to a free lunch.

Employee Activities and Benefits

Employee Appreciation Day—around July of each year a large truck filled with nice ripe watermelons arrives from North Carolina and each employee receives a melon. Pictured here is John Hazel a first-shift welder with his selection in July 2010.

It's watermelon time for all employees: Jon Christianson, welding coordinator in the Compliance Department, is shown here with his selection in July 2010.

149

In November, just in time for each employee's Thanksgiving table, another truck arrives; this one is filled with turkeys, each weighing about twelve pounds. Pictured here receiving their birds are, left to right, Jimmy Campbell and Ricky Still. Both men work in the plate shop.

Pictured from left to right receiving their turkeys are Ron Armistead and Mustafa Abdul-Jalil.

The weather in February 2011 was bitter cold and the shipyard workers were given sweatshirts to help them stay warm. Here are four employees, left to right: Chris Tapia, Marlow Davis, McLendon Blue Jr., and Howard Wheat, receiving their sweatshirts.

year sweatshirts or jackets arrive just in time to help the outside people ward off the northern winds that bring cold temperatures. This past winter was unusually cold, so in February 2011 the yard workers were given hooded sweatshirts to help them stay warm on the many cold and snowy days.

Colonna's Newsletter

In September 1985, *Colonna's Shipyard Inc. Company News* was introduced to the company employees and their families. The following month the word company was dropped and the name became *Colonna's Shipyard Inc. News*.

On February 17, 2006, Volume 1, Issue 1, of what was then known as *Colonna's Newsletter* was published. A small article appearing on page one asked the employees for help in naming the newsletter and stated that the author of the chosen name would receive $50.00. The winning title, chosen by the selection committee was "The Colonna Pilot" which had been submitted by Ms. Sherry Wheatley. The *Colonna Pilot* is published quarterly and is filled with news of employee activities and up-to-date happenings in the shipyard. In earlier years, newsletters were printed under the names of *Colonna's News*, *Colonna's Clipper*, and possibly others.

𝕿𝖍𝖊 𝕮𝖔𝖑𝖔𝖓𝖓𝖆 𝕻𝖎𝖑𝖔𝖙

February 2012   Volume VII, Issue I

Employees of the Year—Selection

June 1986 marked the end of the first year of the Employee of the Month program at Colonna's Shipyard and Norfolk Diesel. It was then time to select the employees of the year. There would be one selection from Colonna's production employees, one selection from Colonna's administrative employees, and the third selection would be from Norfolk Diesel. The employees were graded on work

The houseboat hunting lodge made trips to Buffalo City in the fall of each year for several years. It was around 1935 that a violent hurricane broke it loose from its anchorage in the Indian River and blew it inland. Captain Will tried unsuccessfully to float it back into the river. After several attempts he left it where it is today. This beautiful photo was taken in May 2009.

habits such as productivity, attitude, and attendance, contribution to job effort, cooperation with other employees and safety awareness.

President W. W. (Bill) Colonna Jr. announced the Employees of the Year selections on Thursday, July 3, 1986. The selection from Production was Robert Lett, the Administrative employee of the year was Bruce McCrickard, and Chris Briggs was Norfolk Diesels' employee of the year. Each winner was awarded a two-week all-expenses-paid vacation for his family and himself.

The Crawfish Jamboree

In the spring of 1992, Doug Forrest, executive vice president of Colonna's Shipyard at that time, concocted an idea to make the crew of a Louisiana tugboat feel a little more at home while their boat was in dry dock at Colonna's. Some of the shipyard workers were going to grill some steaks for the visitors from Louisiana. Then someone suggested steaming some "bugs" instead. To those of us not familiar with this Gulf Coast seafood staple "bugs" are crawdads or crawfish. So, the boys from the bayou who were in the Tidewater area for about two months, taught their hosts how to properly prepare those small red carcasses. In

Employee Activities and Benefits

addition to the hundreds of crawfish served at the Colonna houseboat that day, there were several large garbage cans filled with iced cans of beer and soft drinks available for all the guests, which numbered about fifty. The affair has since become an annual outdoor banquet primarily for employees and customers of Colonna's Shipyard. Attendance of the affair, which takes place on the houseboat and the surrounding twenty-four-acre Indian River estate, is by invitation only.

In May 1993, the first annual "Houseboat Cookout," later renamed the "Crawfish Jamboree" took place with about fifty people in attendance. In May 2011, the attendance had risen to approximately seven hundred.

For those lucky enough to receive an invitation, the affair affords a walking tour of the estate where five generations of the Colonna family have lived in the Indian River area of what is now the city of Chesapeake.

The shipyard shindig has not only grown in attendance since its beginning on a rainy day in 1992; but a variety of other foods such as barbecue, coleslaw, baked beans, shrimp, and oysters on the half shell, has joined the "mud bugs." In addition to the great menu, entertainment is now provided by the world famous "Old James River Jazz Band."

Mr. Colonna calls this grand affair the "Crawfish Jamboree." Some others refer to it as the "Mud Bug Party," and still others call it the "Houseboat Cookout." My first attendance of what has been officially named the "Crawfish Jamboree" was Thursday May 7, 2009. My plan was to arrive early and beat some of the expected heavy traffic and park a reasonable distance away. However, my wife had other plans, which amounted to arriving much later. The attendance was in the neighborhood of seven hundred guests and by the time we arrived parking was on the distant shores of the Indian River. I saw exactly 5 people that I knew. The other 695 were complete strangers. However, the food was good and I will say that the main requirement for those in attendance is a hardy appetite. *Bonappetit!*

Colonna's Employee Christmas Party

Colonna's employee Christmas party was held on the top floor of the Crowne Plaza Hotel at 700 Monticello Avenue in Norfolk on Saturday, December 11, 2010. Throughout the year members of the shipyard held various events in order to raise money to pay for prizes that were raffled off the evening of the party. The corporation sponsored the affair.

A buffet was served and all enjoyed good conversation. Dancing was also available for the brave and the young at heart.

Executive Dinner Party—Christmas Celebration—2009

The annual Christmas party for the executives of Colonna's Shipyard was held at the home of Bill and Evelyn Colonna at 316 Kemp Lane, Chesapeake, Virginia, on Saturday evening, December 19, 2009. The autumn weather having

On December 11, 2010, Colonna's employee Christmas Party was held on the top floor of the Crowne Plaza Hotel at 700 Monticello Avenue in Norfolk. Throughout the year the employees held various events in order to raise money to pay for door prizes that were raffled off the evening of the party. The affair was sponsored by the corporation. A buffet was served and good conversation was enjoyed by all. Dancing was also available for the brave and the young at heart.

produced a record amount of rain made for undesirable parking conditions at or near the Colonna home and more inclement weather was forecasted for the day of the affair. In view of those conditions, a decision was made several days before to have the guests use the parking facilities of the nearby Oaklette United Methodist Church. Upon arrival at the church, a shipyard shuttle bus was available to carry the attendees to the Colonna home.

The home, which was beautifully decorated throughout, was filled with shipyard executives and their wives, as well as some of us who were affiliated with the business of the yard in other capacities. The cocktail hour began at 6:00 p.m. and was followed by dinner at 7:00 p.m. The seating arrangement had been predetermined and the guests were assigned to one of several dining areas. Those of us who were not actual employees of the shipyard had dinner in the "Castle Room"

Chimney Corners, the home of Bill and Evelyn Colonna is located at the north end of Kemp Lane on the southern bank of the Indian River, a branch of the Eastern Branch of the Elizabeth River in the city of Chesapeake, Virginia. This is how the house looked in December 2010.

along with Mr. and Mrs. Colonna. The dinner consisted of salad, the main course, desert, and all the wine you cared to drink.

After a leisurely dinner and good conversation everyone adjourned to the main living room where seating was provided for the wonderful entertainment that followed. Mr. Colonna, acting as master of ceremonies, thanked all the executives for their contributions that led to a most successful and profitable year of the shipyard business. He thanked his niece Cheki Thrasher Smith, who not only arranged most that took place and saw to the decorations but also acted as hostess for the evening. She is truly "Uncle Bill's right-hand lady."

The first of the entertainers was Jennifer Lent who is well known for her imitation of Liza Minnelli, daughter of Judy Garland. Ms. Lent sang both holiday and other popular songs. The next member of the team was Kimberly Markham. Ms. Markham may be small but she can really belt out a song and she did just that to several songs throughout the evening. Then there was Roger Cote, a baritone who did justice to many famous songs such as "Ole Man River."

Some of the music was prerecorded, but William Neill provided most music at the piano. Mr. Neill, who is a longtime friend of Mr. and Mrs. Colonna, is employed in the City of Norfolk Commonwealth Attorney's office.

The executive Christmas Dinner is held each December in the home of Bill and Evelyn Colonna on Kemp Lane. The cocktail hour begins at 6:00 p.m. and is followed by dinner at 7:00 p.m. This photograph, which was taken on December 18, 2010, features shipyard executives and their mates in one of several dining areas.

Eventually this very enjoyable evening came to an end. The day had been very rainy and by the time we arrived at the house a light snow was falling and continued throughout the evening; however, the accumulation was light.

This is what took place at the party in the year 2009. This was my first since beginning to write this history of Colonna's Shipyard and its people. Most likely the previous parties were well planned and were also very enjoyable. All of the executive parties in future years will probably be quite similar to this one and will also provide much enjoyment for the guest.

Executive Dinner Party—Christmas—2010

Another wonderful year passed and the annual Christmas party for the executives of Colonna's Shipyard was once again held at the home of Bill and Evelyn Colonna at 316 Kemp Lane, Chesapeake, Virginia on Saturday, December 18,

Those of us who were associated with the shipyard in ways other than employees were seated in the Castle Room with Mr. and Mrs. Colonna.

2010. The weather, being about the same as the previous year, forced the guests to use the parking facilities at the Oaklette United Methodist Church on Indian River Road. Upon arrival at the church, a shipyard shuttle was available to transport the guests directly to the main entrance of the Colonna home.

The home as it was the previous year was beautifully decorated and was filled with shipyard executives and their wives or dates as well as some of us who were affiliated with the business of the yard in other capacities. During the past year I had the privilege of becoming acquainted with more of the executives and as a result felt more at ease than the previous year, which was my first.

The cocktail hour began at 6:00 p.m. and was followed by dinner at 7:00 p.m. As usual the seating was prearranged and the guests were assigned to one of several dining areas. Those of us that were not employees of the shipyard had dinner in the "Castle Room" along with Mr. and Mrs. Colonna. A four-course dinner along with all the wine you cared to drink was served.

After dinner everyone adjourned to the main living area where seating was provided for the entertainment that followed. Shown here, left to right, are Travis Essert, Mr. Colonna's grandson; Roger Cote; Jennifer Lint; and William Neill at the piano. Eventually Martina Essert, Mr. Colonna's granddaughter, joined the entertainers.

After dinner everyone adjourned to the main living area where seating was provided for the entertainment that followed. Mr. Colonna, once again thanked all the executives for their contribution toward another successful business year, after which he introduced the entertainers for the evening. Once again we had the pleasure of listening to the singing of Jennifer Lent and Roger Cote, and the piano music of William Neill. The big surprise of the evening was the addition of entertainers Travis Essert and his sister Martina, grandchildren of Mr. Colonna. All the attendees were pleasantly surprised at the wonderful talent exhibited by these two young people.

During the course of the evening professional photographer Don Beecham used his expertise to record the event for this history and for future generations to enjoy.

As the old saying goes, "All good things must come to an end," and so it was with this very enjoyable evening. As we said "good-bye" and made our way to the shuttle, we encountered a light rain mixed with snow.

Apprenticeship Program

The Registered Apprenticeship Program at Colonna's Shipyard, Inc., is a four-year experience. It attracts talented students in the maritime industry through academic courses and on-the-job training, which can lead to excellent career opportunities with the company.

The program combines college academics, trade theory training, and on-the-job competency experiences. Apprentices are required to complete a minimum of two thousand hours per year of on-the-job training. Apprenticeship graduates earn a nationally recognized journeyman's license.

Participants in the Registered Apprentice Program attend Tidewater Community College and take college-level academic courses. Those courses may be held both at the shipyard and the campus of Tidewater Community College. Participants are employed full-time while they learn, earning a competitive wage and benefits during their four-years of training.

Graduates of the apprenticeship program can earn a career studies certificate or an Associate of Applied Science Degree.

Occupations available in the Colonna's Shipyard Apprenticeship Program at this time include: carpenter, shipfitter, rigger, welder, pipe fitter, inside machinist, outside machinist, and electrician.

Graduates of the Apprenticeship Program.

Chapter IX

Breathtaking Point of Land

The Most Beautiful Point of Land

It was around 1914 that Captain Will Colonna and a friend paddled his canoe about three miles east up the Elizabeth River where he happened upon this piece of real estate. It was breathtaking and he remarked that it was the most beautiful point of land that he had ever seen. The next day, he decided to see if he could find the owner and ask him if he would like to sell the property. This time he climbed into his automobile and drove along the bumpy dirt roads filled with oyster shells

This beautiful home was designed and built in 1920 by Captain Will Colonna, president of Colonna's Shipyard. Construction of his home took one year and cost $126,000. It was built in the Oaklette section of what was then Norfolk County and was about four miles from downtown Norfolk.

to the Oaklette section of Norfolk County where he eventually found Russell Hare, owner of the property. Mr. Hare said he would sell, but made it very clear that he would sell the entire twenty-acre farm, not just the good farmland leaving him with what he called that "no good point of land" on the water where the wind always blew the crops down. Captain Will agreed and bought the entire farm including that "no good point of land" on the water for the sum of $10,000. The purchase included a large two-story house that was sitting on the point. As the story goes, the house at one time involved a doctor and had been used to house "nervous people." Most likely it had been used as an asylum for the care of the mentally ill.

After acquiring this beautiful property Captain Will decided to build his dream home on it. While construction was underway, the family used the house on the point as a temporary place of residence. After completion of what became known as the "big house," the older two-story dwelling was rolled on pine logs from the point to a location that is now 935 St. Lawrence Avenue.

The new house was a large wood frame structure measuring 102 feet in width, 72 feet in depth, and stood two full stories with a finished attic and dormers, which made it, appear to be three stories in height. It was designed by Will Colonna in 1920 and built on the twenty-acre point of land overlooking the Indian River in Oaklette that he had acquired from Russell Hare. The property, which was about four miles east of downtown Norfolk, Virginia, would eventually consist of a forty-eight-room mansion with seven baths and ten fireplaces. Sixteen of the rooms were considerably large and probably the largest was the living room that measured twenty-four by forty-eight feet with a twelve-foot ceiling. The property also consisted of an assortment of other structures that contributed to the comfort and enjoyment of the family. Construction of the house took approximately one year to complete and cost $126,000. The interior of the Colonna's home was furnished with $78,000 worth of beautiful Chippendale furniture.

This big house was typical of that era when large homes were built. Taxes were few and people were allowed to keep most of their hard-earned money. Only the very rich paid any income taxes at all. Just after the end of World War I, the expression was "Let the good times roll!" This was a period of national prosperity, and there was no reason to believe that it would ever come to an end, but come to an end it did. In 1929, the stock market crashed and the Great Depression that followed lasted for ten very long years. During the Depression years, the expression was, "Mister can you spare a dime?"

This forty-eight-room house burned twice. The first fire occurred in 1923 and the house was rebuilt. After the second fire in 1925, the house was beyond repair.

This beautiful home burned twice—the first time was in 1923, when it partially burned and was rebuilt with a flat roof. It never looked the same after that fire and the repairs that followed. The second time it burned was on a cold winter night in 1925 while the family was attending a silent movie in downtown Norfolk. The Fire Department was unable to extinguish the fire because the river was frozen and at low tide. In those days, the Fire Department fought fire by placing suction hoses in the river. Captain Colonna often said that both fires were set and he knew who set them, but there was no way of proving it. Most likely we will never know for sure. The guilty person or persons had to be filled with hate and as a result of some misunderstanding, held a grudge against Mr. Colonna.

There was very little insurance on the house. In those days people didn't bother with insuring their properties and it was not a requirement for obtaining a loan. After the second fire the house was never rebuilt; however, the property still remains in the family and some new things have been added. In addition to all the trees that were on the property when Captain Will bought it, he purchased 101 pecan trees through the mail from the state of Georgia. Eventually they produced a large harvest of nuts in the fall of each year and the children were kept busy picking them up off the ground.

Captain Will's Hunting Lodge

When Captain Will Colonna, assisted by his four young daughters, built the houseboat in the 1920s, he never gave it a name, a paddle, or an engine. It was built using a Chesapeake and Ohio Railway car float pontoon barge as the hull that probably dated back to the very early 1900s. He had no drawings to follow, but designed it himself as he went along. What he created was a boxy boat that was about forty feet by thirty-six feet with two stories, each with covered, wraparound decks. He included doors and windows on all four sides. All the pine timber used in its construction came from the local woodlands.

Why did he build this floating house? He did it mostly to host business associates and friends. In the fall of each year, the steam tug named for Carl D. Colonna (built in 1891) towed her for two days, transporting a group of hunters down the Albemarle Sound west of the Outer Banks, to the logging community of Buffalo City in Dare County, North Carolina. Buffalo City was situated on Mill Tail Creek near East Lake. By 1927, most of the timber had been harvested and the three things still growing strong around Buffalo City were black bears, big bucks, and plenty of white lightning.

The first time the bootleggers saw this monstrosity flying the American flag and the decks lined with men holding shotguns, they thought for sure that they were a bunch of revenuers that had come to destroy their stills. After finding that the men had come just to hunt wild life, the hunters and bootleggers became friends. As a matter of fact each morning at daybreak a gallon of corn liquor was mysteriously placed on the deck of the houseboat. When Captain Will asked the locals where it came from their answer was always the same, "It was left by an old lady from the village who was dressed in shaggy clothes and was referred to as the sea hag."

Once the houseboat arrived at Buffalo City it remained for the entire hunting season. This meant that those who wanted to commute from Norfolk had to travel

In the 1920s Captain Will, assisted by his four young daughters, built the houseboat hunting lodge. In the fall of each year the steam tug named for Carl D. Colonna spent two days transporting hunters down to Buffalo City in Dare County, North Carolina.

by automobile, ferry boats, and many miles of unpaved roads. So when a prospective hunter arrived he was always tired from the long uncomfortable journey.

During the daylight hours the hunters steered canoes or small flat-bottom boats equipped with outboard motors through the swamplands in search of game. For about eight autumns the houseboat made its annual migration to Mill Tail Creek. Throughout the years the hunters brought hundreds of deer, bear, and squirrel back to Norfolk.

By all calculations the nautical hunting lodge made its last trip to Buffalo City in the fall of 1933 and returned to the Norfolk area in the spring of 1934. In 1935, a violent hurricane broke the houseboat loose from its anchorage in the Indian River and blew it about a quarter mile inland. Although the barge was moved by the hurricane, the houseboat sitting on it was so well constructed that it was unharmed. Soon afterwards Captain Will tried to float it back to the river. He built a couple of dirt dams across the cove, waited for spring water to fill the pond, and then floated it a few feet downstream. He then proceeded to take the top dam out and rebuild it a little farther down. Eventually Captain Will got tired of building dams and left the boat where it is today. The float, which was

After the hunt in Buffalo City, the hunters gathered around the houseboat. This photograph shows deer skins hanging on the porch, a deer, hunting dogs, canoes, outboard motors, and flat-bottom boats, to the left is a sea sled turned on its side with the bottom showing. Emmett Jones (Jonsie) the cook, can be seen standing on the porch. He is the man wearing a white apron.

built of heavy creosote timbers is still underneath and resting on the bottom of the pond. There is a spring that feeds into the area surrounding the houseboat. Although the Elizabeth River is salt water, the pond around the houseboat is fresh water. In walking across the bridge from the land to the houseboat it is fascinating to stop and watch the large turtles and fish that make their homes in the pond.

The houseboat remained in the Colonna family until 1948. They then sold it and approximately 4 acres surrounding the pond to Bill and Ruby Mansfield for the sum of $5,000. The couple planned to live on board just long enough to build a house on the land nearby. However, they continued to live on the boat for thirty years and raised two daughters. They never did fulfill their original plan to build a home near the houseboat. The Mansfield family returned to conventional residential living in 1978. In August 1978, W. W. Colonna Jr. bought the houseboat and 3.7 acres from Bill and Ruby Mansfield for $100,000.

Upon examination of the interior he found that the houseboat had been changed somewhat, but still retained many of its assets. Originally the interior was pretty rough; many of the walls and floors were unfinished and there was no

This photograph shows part of the logging operation in Buffalo City.

insulation. After all it was a floating hunting lodge for a bunch of men. The outside was presentable but the inside was quite primitive.

Today when entering the houseboat a visitor is asked to sign the log, which can be found on a table in the entrance hall or should I say passageway. A washer and drier have been installed in one of the upstairs bedrooms. Leather armchairs are available for those who wish to sit back and enjoy a television program or sporting event. Brass spittoons sit beside each door. There are two in the second story saloon. Bottles of Jack Daniels and Johnny Walker Red fill the shelves where corn liquor once was stored. The main upstairs attraction is the player piano. Most of the songs became popular during the Great Depression era. The instrument is an original 1928 Weber. Like many of us it can now lay claim to being an octogenarian.

Today the houseboat is used for small socials with family, friends, clubs, and business associates. The interior is a mix of nautical and 1920 furnishings. The heavily treed surroundings make it the perfect location for small weddings and parties. Standing near the water's edge and gazing at the old boat you can almost hear the sounds of the big brass bands from bygone days and see beautiful ladies in large hoop skirts holding fancy parasols, strolling along the porches, and sipping mint juleps.

Although Captain Will never gave it a name, most everybody in the city of Chesapeake has heard about the unusual, yet beautiful houseboat that eventually acquired the name "Colonna Houseboat." In the year 2000 the Chesapeake Cosmopolitan Club even selected the Colonna Houseboat as the subject for its annual commemorative Christmas ornament.

Buffalo City, North Carolina

So what ever happened to Buffalo City? That was a question that W. W. Colonna Jr. often thought about. He had accompanied his father Captain Will on several of the hunting trips when he was just a young lad. In November 1987, he decided to make a return trip to see what things were like. He found that Buffalo City as he remembered it was no longer there. It had been reclaimed by the swamplands. In the early 1900s it was a thriving lumber town with a population between a thousand and fifteen hundred people. In its heyday miles of railroad tracks were laid through the swamp and trains powered by steam engines were used to haul the harvest of logs to the loading docks where barges were waiting to carry them to Norfolk and northern cities. With the onset of the lumber business, the town called Buffalo City sprang up in what had previously been nothing more than woods and swampland.

It soon became a rough wild town located on the northern side of Mill Tail Creek about three and one half miles from the entrance to the Alligator River in Dare County, which in the early 1900s was also referred to as the East Lake area. The town's general appearance was much like that of an old western town that you may have seen in early cowboy movies. Most of the buildings were of board and batten construction and a railroad ran down the center of what could be called the main street, such as it was. Buffalo City did have its own hotel and general store. The families lived in individual houses on streets that had been laid off and called First, Second, and Third Streets; however, different nationalities and ethnic groups did live together in separate sections of the town. The work force was made up of native Carolinians, along with large groups of Italians, Russians, and Blacks.

There were no state regulated laws so the citizens took it upon themselves to enforce some sort of law and order whether it was right or wrong. There was a whipping post in the town and it was said that the last person to be whipped in public was the owner of the general store. Supposedly he made grocery deliveries to women at their homes when the husbands were at work in the swamp or mill. Apparently some of the wives kept the grocery money for themselves and made payment with certain personal favors. The grocer eventually gained the reputation of being a womanizer, which in turn gained him a trip to the town whipping post.

An often-told story was that on at least one occasion six persons that had been labeled as troublemakers were forced into a building at gunpoint and told if they came out they would be shot. The doors and windows were boarded and nailed shut; gasoline was then thrown on the building and it was set on fire. There were also stories about men going to work in the swamp in early morning and not re-turning home at the end of the day. The assumption was that they were killed and buried in the swamp.

A close look along the edge of Mill Tail Creek would often reveal thin rope or cord tied to cypress knees, trees, or tree roots and disappearing into the dark cypress waters where the other end was attached to a five gallon jug of corn or rye whiskey. This served two purposes. One was to hide the whiskey and the other was to make it easily accessible. Many years later some of the forgotten jugs were found and connoisseurs of good whiskey said the contents were just great.

W. W. Colonna Jr.'s return trip in November 1987 began with a drive to East Lake west of Manteo, North Carolina, where his party was met by local resident and guide Alvin Ambrose Jr. The group proceeded on a tour through the swamp where they soon found remains of the old Buffalo City sawmill and piers on Mill Tail Creek, where Captain Will Colonna use to tie up his houseboat hunting lodge in the 1920s and early 1930s. The remains of Buffalo City and Claude Duvall's general store were located several hundred yards north of the old sawmill site. It was still possible to follow the remains of the tram railroad beds through much of the swamp. Traveling approximately three-quarters of a mile east up Mill Tail Creek there was a piece of high ground called "Sandy Ridge" where reportedly five families once lived and made their living by farming, hunting, splitting wood-en shingles, logging, and making moon shine. Soon after the turn of the nineteenth to the twentieth century they made most of their money from the sale of corn or

This is part of the crew with engine No. 5 at Buffalo City. Most of them look too well dressed to be workmen (maybe they were in their Sunday-go-to-meeting clothes). Also several small children can be seen in this photograph.

rye whiskey to the outside world. Then the family feuding began and the intensity became so great that there were reported shootouts. Eventually things got so bad the families one by one pulled-up stakes and moved.

Upon visiting the north side of Mill Tail Creek, an ancient cemetery was discovered. It was well hidden by weeds, vines, and young trees, making it hard to find. But once found, it proved to be very large and provided the final resting place for former residents and perhaps a few others. Most of the graves were marked with old ballast stones that most likely came from wooden sailing vessels of earlier times. Most graves were marked with both head and footstones and some with only one stone. Then there were sunken graves with no markers. Several large colored stones were found piled on the north side of the cemetery; no one knew exactly what purpose if any that they served.

It proved to be a lovely day. Everyone was outfitted in old clothes and boots that provided protection as well as comfort for the tour. Although the area is noted for snakes, none were encountered; however, one black bear was seen from a distance. Information received from the local folks say that there are alligators in the swamp that measure twelve to fourteen feet in length.

Some of the present-day natives claim to be descendants of the "Lost Colony." Remember when Governor White returned to Roanoke Island in 1590 all he found of the colony was the word *Croatoan* carved on a tree. Thus the name given

The Colonna Houseboat.

to the colony that disappeared was the "Lost Colony." Even to this day some people believe the colonists married into the local Indian tribes. Close observation of present-day natives of this area reveal distinguishing characteristics of the early American natives. So what we have here is what is known as "unwritten history or word of mouth," which has been passed from one generation to the next. In many cases architectural digs have proved this type of history to be true.

Chimney Corners

Any history involving the Colonna family would not be complete without a few well-chosen words about the old home on what became known as Kemp Lane. In my youth I remember Kemp Lane as a small, unpaved road that ran perpendicular to Indian River Road. It was probably the width of an automobile. Actually it was more like a path through a cornfield, for each side of the road consisted of corn as high as an elephant's eye—there were no houses until reaching near the waters of the Indian River. Beginning in 1903 Arrelious W. Kemp owned and farmed about forty-two acres of land in that area.

Try to imagine, the year is 1789 and George Washington is the first president of the United States. Sitting along the edge of what would become known as the Indian River is a twenty-by-forty-foot gambrel-roof house that will, in later years,

This painting by Casey Holtzinger depicts a circa 1789 Elizabeth River farmhouse. In 1860 this house was moved one hundred feet northwest from its original location. Since its relocation in 1860 it has had five additions as follows: a carriage house, basement section, great room-porch and basement, kitchen, and a three-story brick addition.

be moved a distance of about one hundred feet northwest from its existing location. In 1904, after having been moved, Arrelious W. Kemp bought this small house. The lower brick section that is attached to the back of the house was built around 1916 or 1917 by Mr. Kemp. It was around that time that the automobile was beginning to come into its own; however, many people still depended on the old-fashioned horse and carriage. So this section of the house was known as the carriage house.

In 1931 Mr. Kemp sold the home to Dean and Mollie Preston. Mr. Preston was a pharmacist and owned Preston's Pharmacy in South Norfolk. Shortly after 1931 and for a number of years after the house was referred to as the "Preston house." While it was under ownership of the Preston family a fair amount of work was accomplished towards its restoration. There was no chimney on what is now the north end; so Mr. Preston had one added.

The old home has had several owners since the Preston family. Among them were: Vernon Forehand who served as city attorney for the City of South Norfolk and another was retired United States Air Force Lieutenant Colonel Peters and Mrs. Peters. This home located at 316 Kemp Lane in the city of Chesapeake, Virginia, is now the residence of Bill and Evelyn Colonna.

Their home was built in five different time periods beginning with the 1789 two-story gambrel-roof section and ending with the 1990 three-story Georgian colonial addition on the north end of the house. The inside of the house with its many rooms, stairs, doors—and even an elevator—built in different time periods is most interesting and can be very challenging for a first-time visitor who may be trying to find his or her way around.

The various architectural time periods found in this one house makes the outside just as fascinating as the inside. Actually it appears to be a cluster of fine homes nestled together. The exterior of the house looks quite amazing when illuminated at night for the multitude of shadows can cause one's imagination to run wild. If you look hard enough you may see George, the father of our country, ride up on horseback.

The Hodges House

It was in 1818 that John Hodges purchased 150 acres along the Eastern Branch of the Elizabeth River. With each passing of ownership throughout the years the original plantation was subdivided and sold little by little until just a small part is left today.

The Hodges house stands on Indian River Road across from Riverside Cemetery—just a short distance from the entrance to Colonna's Shipyard. W. W. Colonna Jr. acquired the property in 1978, from the estate of Dr. Green, a local physician.

Recall, the Hodges house first entered our story around 1883/1884 when Benjamin A. Colonna laid out a proposed road from the Berkley Ferry to the south end of the Campostella Bridge and again in 1885 when there was a disagreement between the Berkley Ferry Company and the Campostella Bridge Company about the course that the proposed road should take between the Hodges house and the foot of the Campostella Bridge.

Not knowing the age of the old house, Mr. Colonna contacted Colonial Williamsburg and inquired about having someone from their architectural research group to come and see about dating the structure. On April 6, 1978, Paul E. Buchanan, director of architectural research for the Colonial Williamsburg Foundation, visited the Hodges house. The purpose of his visit was to gather on-site information that could be used in dating the old structure. His report included the following information: The house is a typical simple Federal style residence. It is a two-and-one-half-story building with a full cellar. It is of the double-pile side passage plan with two interior end chimneys, centered on the rooms. The end opposite

Hodges House

the passage is brick. The other walls are beaded weatherboards, now covered with asbestos siding. The brickwork on the north and west walls are Flemish bond, but on the east and south walls it is three-course American bond. The brick joints were tooled with a 1/8″ x 1/8″ fillet groove, similar to most eighteen-century brick joints. The house has a gable roof. Mr. Buchanan said, "Using only architectural features and details, I would date the building between 1810 and 1820, probably nearer to 1820." The building was retrimmed with new interior woodwork, on the first and second floors, between 1830 and 1845. The third floor still has most of its original trim. Some minor alterations were made in the late nineteenth century and the cellar, kitchen, and dining areas had some alterations in the 1930s.

To the east of the house is a brick garage that was built as the plantation office around 1820. The chimney and large cooking fireplace have been removed to allow the installation of a garage door. The floor and ceiling line have been lowered about two feet. This building was connected to the main house in the late nineteenth century.

This would suggest that John Hodges probably built the house after he obtained the property in 1818. The interior alterations mentioned were most likely made by Hodges who acquired the "Mansion House," after his mother's death.

It has been said that possibly George Washington visited the Hodges house on two different occasions meeting with the previous residents of the house. If Mr. Buchanan's report that the house was built around 1820 is correct or near correct, then Washington could not have visited the house because he died in 1799.

Chapter X

Tales of Old Berkley

The Hardy Tract

Any mention of Berkley generally brings to mind memories of the "old Hardy Tract" and the large plantation house that was built by the Herbert family in the 1600s. I will not attempt to write a complete history of the Hardy house and the surrounding area for I did that in one of my earlier books. However, I would like to include information about some of the local families that possibly were there in 1875 when young Charles J. Colonna built his shipyard nearby.

In the 1700s a drawbridge was located at one end of what later became South Main Street. This bridge, which served as a means of thoroughfare for carriages, connected what was then known as Washington to Norfolk Town. After removal of the drawbridge, a foot ferry that was operated by E. L. Bell was established at that location and remained in operation until after the Berkley Bridge was built in 1916. Mr. Bell and his family lived in the Hardy house in those days.

Edna Bell and two of her sisters were born in this house on the banks of the Elizabeth River; Edna eventually married J. O. Morgan who was a native of Berkley. Morgan remembered going to school in the three-story house before the public school was built on Sixth Street.

On January 11, 1892, the Ryland Institute, which was an all-girl school, was incorporated by an act of the General Assembly of Virginia. The school took up residence in the old house. Young Morgan remembered seeing the girls in their black hats and black gowns.

It was a daily pastime for the children of that era to run through the fields and play along the waterfront near the old house for no Hardy had lived there for years. The house looked old and worn out; no repairs had been accomplished for a very long time. The grand old lady stood on a promontory with a good command of the Elizabeth River.

It was known that the Hardy house had an underground tunnel and the old graveyard, which was situated about two hundred feet from the house stood in a group of small trees and was surrounded by a variety of shrubs. The graves had been long forgotten and were overgrown with weeds and honeysuckle. The vaults, however, had withstood time exceedingly well for the rounded tops showed about a foot out of the ground. There was a large opening in the end of one of them and you could jump in and land on the floor of the vault where you could see headstones and slabs, and quite a few human bones.

Throughout the years the Hardy house continued to deteriorate. It became a haven for drunks and the homeless. Many fires were set within its walls. On December 15, 1948, this historic property consisting of twenty-eight acres fronting 1,225 feet on the Berkley side of the Elizabeth River was purchased by Colonna's Shipyard for the reported sum of $50,000. This is part of the property that was deeded from the Hardy Homestead Corporation to the Pescara Land Corporation on September 9, 1907, and was conveyed to George W. Norris on October 28, 1909.

The transaction was handled by George Hope Taylor, realtor. The sellers of the property were the Girard Trust Company and Hubert A. Jordan, of Philadelphia, trustees under the will of the late George W. Norris.

Soon after, the old house sustained one last fire that sealed its fate for all time. A young future scientist from the local neighborhood using flammable materials controlled by a timer, sat patiently on the front porch of his home and awaited the explosion that ignited the final conflagration. Afterwards, being completely beyond repair, the once elegant plantation home that faced the Elizabeth River was demolished in early 1951.

Enough of the original bricks from the former rambling three-story structure were salvaged to build a wall around a small park that includes plaques memorializing General Douglas MacArthur's mother Pinky who had been born in the house. In September 1951, the general, his wife, and son Arthur came to Norfolk to dedicate the park.

In 1875, Charles J. Colonna's first ship repair facility was founded on property leased from the Hardy family and located directly across from their plantation home. Today, Colonna's Shipyard is still a close neighbor and is even within walking distance of what became the town of Berkley in 1890. Some members of the Colonna family as well as friends and business associates made their homes in that nearby community. Throughout the earlier years many interesting tales involving members of the family and others have been passed down and hopefully are worthy of sharing with the readers of this history.

Home of Carl and Pearl Colonna

Several of our stories involve Carl Colonna Sr., his wife Pearl Sykes, and eventually their son Carl Colonna Jr. who in his youth was known as "Carlie Boy." Carl Colonna and Pearl Sykes had been married at *Pescara*, the old colonial farmhouse on shipyard property on March 18, 1903. In the early years of their marriage they lived in a house at what is now 232 Hardy Avenue. Most of the early homes were heated by potbellied stoves that burned wood and coal and later some of them used stoves that were fueled by kerosene. Needless to say those early stoves could heat only one or two rooms at the most. The other rooms were closed off during the cold winter months. When spending time in the unheated rooms, it became necessary to wear additional heavy clothing in order to try to escape the discomfort brought on by the cold.

After experiencing several record-breaking cold winters, Carl decided to have a coal-fired furnace installed in the basement and cast-iron radiators in all the rooms of the house. When the installation was complete, a fire was built in the furnace and soon afterwards a feeling of warmth that Pearl had never associated with their home before, began to spread throughout all the rooms. After a while she was actually able to remove her coat and then her sweater. She was so pleased that she just walked from room to room holding her arms over her head and waving them back and forth in a display of comfort and happiness. Of course several times a day the furnace would have to be fed with coal and then there was the job of removing the ashes and banking the fire at night; however, the comfort that it provided made all this work worthwhile.

Carl owned another house at what is now 224 Indian River Road. There was nothing particularly grand about the place. It was just an older two-story wood frame house; however, it was capable of providing a comfortable livable place for a family. About this time Carl and Pearl were devoted members of the Episcopal Church in Berkley. Although Carl couldn't sing he was a member of the church choir. The preacher and others realized this so Carl did not sing along with the others but was allowed to end each hymn with a very loud "Amen!" That was his thing and he loved doing it. Suddenly the spirit moved Carl and he decided to give the house on Indian River Road to the preacher. After doing that all the church members as well as others praised him and continuously remarked that he was a very kind and generous man. But his brothers Will and Ben commented, "That he wasn't as nice as people thought that he simply gave the house to the preacher so they would let him remain in the choir."

Later, probably about the mid-1930s, Carl was a Sunday school teacher at the Episcopal Church. His nephew young Billy Colonna having been baptized there was now attending Sunday school. One Sunday his Uncle Carl was teaching from the Book of Jonah. Remember, Jonah was swallowed by a large fish and lived in its belly for three days and three nights, after which the fish vomited him up on the beach. For some strange reason, Billy who usually remained quiet, spoke up and said, "I don't believe that." His uncle told him to stay after class that he wanted to talk to him. So after the others left class Carl tried to convince him that the story was true and Billy remained firm in his conviction that the story was not true and he just didn't believe it. This made his Uncle Carl mad and he said, "When I get to the shipyard tomorrow I am going to tell your father." So sure enough on Monday Carl went to the office and told Billy's father, Will. Will looked up at him and said, "Carl I don't believe it either." Of course this made Carl even madder, but Billy was off the hook and probably Carl never mentioned that story again.

Carl Colonna Jr. who served many years as general superintendent of Colonna's Shipyard told the next group of tales. He had the reputation of being a very fine man and was also known to be a very smart man as well. He shared these stories with his cousin Bill many years after the facts.

Carlie Boy and Willie Bernard

As was previously mentioned, Carl Colonna Sr. and Pearl were members of the Episcopal Church in Berkley and so "Carlie Boy" who was born on June 26, 1905, also became a member of the church. He had to attend church every Sunday with his parents. He was expected to be quiet, be polite, and sit in the pew and listen to the preacher. He usually had a friend sitting close by and if they each had a pencil and a scrap of paper they would pass notes back and forth. If they did not have paper to write on they would write in the margin of the hymnals and pass those to each other. In later years after "Carlie Boy" became a grown man his mother Pearl had one of the hymnals that he had written in the margin. It simply said, "had a fight with Willie Bernard yesterday, I won, I think."

The Perfect Trick

Their home at 232 Hardy Avenue had stairs leading from the first floor to the second floor and continuing on to the attic. This gave the house the appearance of being three stories high. One day Carlie was up in the attic and heard voices downstairs. He looked over the rail and saw his mother talking to the maid. The maid was on her hands and knees with a bucket of water beside her, a brush in one hand and a bar of soap in the other hand. She was scrubbing the floor beneath the stairwell. "Carlie Boy" looked around and saw a stack of old books in the attic that looked to be about six feet high and in that stack was a really large book about fifteen inches square and four inches thick. It was a very heavy book. Suddenly a devilish idea popped into his young head. He took the book off the pile, walked over to the rail, held it perfectly parallel to the floor below, made sure no one was standing directly under him and released the book from what amounted to about three stories in height. When it hit the first floor beside the maid there was a loud sound like someone had fired a shotgun. The trick had worked perfectly. When he looked again he saw that the maid had fainted. The bucket had turned over, water was all over the floor, the bar of soap was in one place and the brush was in another. The maid had collapsed face down in the soapy water with her arms out to her side and her legs spread out at the back. As he looked over the rail the next scene he saw became imbedded into his mind forever. It was one that he would never forget for the rest of his life. His mother looked straight up and simply said, "We will attend to this matter when your father gets home." He knew what he was in for. Neither he nor his mother mentioned it for the rest of the day but he knew that the executioner would be home later and he knew what to expect. There is no doubt that young Carlie got a spanking like he had never had before, and the maid probably never returned to that house again.

Berkley's Beautiful Girl

The next story is about the most beautiful girl in all of Berkley. Everyone agreed that she was the prettiest girl that they had ever seen. She attended church regularly, she was very proper, well mannered, mild, and polite and on top of all those remarkable traits, she was also very smart. There was no doubt about it no one could match her, she would be the best possible catch on the face of the earth.

Everyone loved her and Carl Colonna Jr., now a young man, had thoughts about trying to court her and eventually becoming engaged. One day a social was held at someone's house and the number of attendees was quite large. Between the kitchen and dining room was a swinging door. A lot of people were standing around in the dining room socializing and eating snacks. This beautiful young lady happened to be standing near the swinging door when someone opened it to bring more food out of the kitchen to the dining room. The door struck her on the elbow and inflicted excruciating pain. It was so sudden and so painful that this most perfect young lady forgot all her nice qualities and let go of a string of curse words that would put a drunken sailor to shame. Realizing what she had said, she stopped suddenly, but it was too late. All those years spent building that wonderful reputation was abolished in a matter of seconds, and all those present saw that Berkley's most beautiful and perfect girl was not perfect after all.

The Fat Lady

The next tale of Berkley is not meant to make fun of any group or class of people. It is just the way it was in those earlier years. In the days before home refrigerators most families owned what was called an icebox. It was a wooden box that held a block of ice and a drip pan was place underneath to catch the water from the melting ice. There was really no way to keep foods that required refrigeration and there was no such thing as frozen foods. People made several trips each week to the neighborhood grocery store. Some families shopped daily. The typical grocery of those days was a small store with an awning across the front and on the sidewalk were coups with live chickens in them. There were also baskets of fresh produce such as collard and other greens in season and in the summer months there could be found an ample supply of homegrown watermelons and cantaloupes. Usually the floor inside was covered with sawdust and the more modern stores were equipped with ceiling fans that provided a small amount of coolness during the hot weather. In winter warmth was supplied by the burning of coal and wood in the familiar potbellied stove.

Carl Colonna Jr. used to tell the tale of the fat lady who lived in Berkley. She was so obese that it was very difficult for her to walk and carry a market basket filled with groceries. She like others during those earlier days needed to make several trips each week to the local grocery store. Being unable to carry her market basket when it was filled, she would hire the same little boy each day and give him a dime to go to the store with her and carry her basket back home. On Saturdays and during the summer months a group of boys hung around outside the grocery store. Most likely they were trying to make money carrying filled market baskets home for patrons of the store. At this particular time the little boy had gone to the fat lady's house and was walking behind her with the empty market basket. As they approached the store this group of boys in front commenced chanting "here comes da fat lady, here comes da fat lady and the closer she got the louder they chanted. As she waddled in front of the store, the little boy walking behind her carrying her basket yelled out "Y'all can kiss da fat lady's A—." He actually thought he was being nice to the fat lady by yelling at the other boys. She walked a few more steps; the little boy punched her on the thigh, she turned and looked down at him, he grinned from ear to ear and said, "Hey fat lady didn't I tell 'em sumpen, didn't I tell 'em sumpen fat lady?" This is just one of the many things that possibly happened in walking to or from a grocery store in Berkley.

Bellamy Avenue

This next tale of Berkley occurred at the home of Bill Colonna's grandparents George W. and Pearle Daughtry. The Daughtrys built their home at 117 Bellamy Avenue in Berkley and lived there for a countless number of years. After their children grew up and had children of their own, the home on Bellamy Avenue became a favorite family gathering place each year on Christmas Day.

Our story took place on a Sunday afternoon after church. It was one of those hot Berkley summers before the days of home air conditioning. Pearle, a group of her lady friends, and her young daughter Esther, seeking relief from the heat of the house, had gathered on the front porch with hand-held fans. They were fanning themselves and were deeply engaged in conversation. Suddenly all the talk stopped and each lady covered her face with her fan. Esther said, "Mother what is happening here, what is wrong?" Her mother said, "Just keep quiet for a minute and I will tell you." Esther looked up and saw a lady walking down the sidewalk. After the lady passed, Esther's mother told her the lady was a divorcee that lived in the next block and that proper ladies did not speak to divorced women and that was the reason the ladies used their fans to cover their faces. Times certainly have changed.

What was Berkley Really Like?

So what was Berkley really like? We know that it had its beginning in the 1600s with the Herbert family. However, I would like to describe the community that existed when Bill Colonna and I were youngsters. When the streets were originally laid out and houses were built there were wide alleys behind all the houses. Those alleys served many purposes but mostly they were there for the delivery of coal and wood in winter and ice in summer. Also, many other deliveries such as groceries were made to the back of the house instead of the front and some of the houses even had a horse stall that could be accessed from the alley. In those years there were many street vendors with their horse-drawn wagons. Among them were the produce and certain days of the week fish peddlers. One regular vendor was a Mr. Goodman. He had a horse and wagon and would walk the streets of Berkley, selling vegetables, fresh eggs, and also, mostly on Fridays, he sold fresh fish. The iceman made deliveries six days a week, Mondays through Saturdays. As has been stated before, there were no refrigerators. Most people had an icebox. A square sign with the numbers 25, 50, 75, and 100 was placed in one of the windows to let the iceman know how many pounds of ice to deliver. The number at the top of the sign indicated the number of pounds of ice the customer wanted that day. As was previously related most people had to make several trips to the grocery store each week. Also most local dairies made home deliveries of milk and other dairy products. The Blue Law was in effect in those days and that meant that all the stores were required by law to close on Sunday. That was the way it was in the Berkley of those days.

BIBLIOGRAPHY

Couper, William. *The V.M.I. New Market Cadets.* Charlottesville, VA: The Michie Company, 1933.

Graham, Martin F. *Blue and Grey,* Lincolnwood, IL: Publications International, Ltd., 2006.

Harper, Raymond L. *Making of America: Chesapeake, Virginia.* Charleston, SC: Arcadia Publishing, 2002.

_____. *A History of Chesapeake Virginia,* Charleston, SC: The History Press, 2008.

Tyler, Lynn Gardiner, ed. *Men of Mark in Virginia: Ideals of American Life; a Collection of Biographies of the Leading Men in the State.* Washington, D.C.: Men of Mark Publishing Company, 1909.

Newspapers (Listed Chronologically)

The Norfolk Ledger-Dispatch, Tuesday, April 14, 1914.

The Norfolk Landmark, Tuesday, October 7, 1924.

The Portsmouth Star, Sunday January 23, 1938.

The Norfolk Virginian-Pilot, Thursday January 13, 1949.

The Norfolk Virginian-Pilot, Monday December 7, 1959.

The Norfolk Virginian-Pilot, Monday January 11, 1960.

The Norfolk Virginian-Pilot, March 9, 1961.

The Norfolk Ledger-Dispatch, March 20, 1961.

The Norfolk Virginian-Pilot, June 30, 1961.

The Ports of Greater Hampton Roads, 1963.

The Norfolk Ledger-Dispatch, June 17, 1963.

The Norfolk Ledger-Star, Wednesday, March 10, 1971.

The Norfolk Ledger-Star, Tuesday, March 23, 1971.

The Times Advocate, Friday, March 21, 1980.

The Virginian-Pilot, June 17, 1986.

Maritime Bulletin-Hampton Roads Maritime Association, July 1986.

The Virginian-Pilot, February 8, 1990.

The Virginian-Pilot and The Ledger-Star, Saturday, March 31, 1990.

The Ledger-Star, Wednesday, April 25, 1990.

The Virginian-Pilot, Thursday, April 26, 1990.

The Virginian-Pilot, Thursday, May 17, 1990.

The Virginian-Pilot and The Ledger-Star, Monday June 11, 1990.

Maritime Bulletin, September 1990.

The Virginian-Pilot and The Ledger-Star, Monday September 17, 1990.

The Virginian-Pilot and The Ledger-Star, October 17, 1990.

The Virginian-Pilot, Wednesday, December 5, 1990.

The Virginian-Pilot and The Ledger-Star, Sunday December 30, 1990.

The Virginian-Pilot, August 19, 1998.

The Virginian-Pilot, August 24, 1998.

The Virginian-Pilot, Tuesday, November 7, 2000.

The Virginian-Pilot, Saturday, May 12, 2001.

The Virginian-Pilot, August 4, 2004.

The Virginian-Pilot, Friday, July 28, 2006.

The Virginian-Pilot Compass, Sunday May 11, 2008.

The Virginian-Pilot, Friday, October 31, 2008.

The Virginian-Pilot, Saturday, February 28, 2009.

The Virginian-Pilot, Thursday, June 12, 2009.

The Virginian-Pilot, Wednesday, August 19, 2009.

The Virginian-Pilot, Sunday, April 25, 2010.

Periodicals, Minutes, and Miscellany

Clerk's Office Circuit Court of Northampton County, Commonwealth of Virginia, Deed Book 37, pages 675–676 and Deed Book 38, pages 555-556 and 631-632.

Battle of New Market (May 15, 1864) Official Records, Virginia Military Institute.

Benjamin A. Colonna Letters, Volume V-E July 18, 1878–May 13, 1879.

Biography of Benjamin Azariah Colonna: Volume I, March 1903; Volume II, March 1986. Accomack County, Virginia, and Washington, D.C.

Marine Iron Works Company, Inc., Director and Stockholder Minutes, December 5, 1917–January 14, 1922, Norfolk, Virginia.

Colonna's Shipyard, Inc., Director and Stockholder Minutes, December 31, 1921–January 7, 1957; February 6, 1968–October 9, 1973; February 1, 1974–January 10,1983; January 11, 1988–June 19,1989; June 30,1989–May 23, 1990; July 6, 1990–January 13, 1992; April 1992–October 1993.

Colonna Papers: Volume I, July 1988; Volume II, May 1996. Norfolk, VA: Colonna's Shipyard, Inc.

Colonna, Charles Jones, Family Bible.

INDEX

A

A. Brooke Taylor (fishing vessel), 84
A. Vernon McNeal (fishing vessel), 54
Accomack County, Virginia, 10, 13, 22
Albero, Carl, 18, 133
Ambrose, Alvin, Jr., 170
Andrew J. Barberi (ferry), 122, 123
Apprentice Program, 161
Argonaut (container ship), 137
Arna (tramp steamer), 64
Atlantic Fishing Company, 70, 71, 73, 76
Automobile, Charles J. Colonna's, 57

B

B. O. Colonna (fishing vessel), 70
Ballard, Captain, 125
Bankruptcy, 11, 60, 97, 100, 102, 103,
    105, 132, 137
Barnes, S. D., 63
Barque Belstone, (sailing vessel), 52
Barraud, E., 41
Beasily, "Tato," 139
Bell, E. L., 176
Bell, Edna, 176
Berkley, 6, 10, 12, 26, 36, 39, 40, 41, 53,
    54, 58, 70, 75, 78, 86, 89, 91, 100,
    103, 116, 121, 127, 128, 176, 177,
    178, 179, 180, 181, 182, 183
Berkley Ferry, 174
Berkley, Waverly Lee, III, 18, 13
Berkley, Waverly Lee, Jr., 46
Bernagozzi, Hugo, 131
Bibb, CSS, 15, 23, 24, 25

Boggs, Sarah, 13
Boykin, Kelly, 123
Brisebois, Lucy, 10
Britton, Ellen, 10
Brustar, William S., 54
Buffalo City, North Carolina, 165, 166,
    167, 168, 169, 170, 171, 172
Burkart, Ray, 132

C

C. C. Sadler (schooner), 22
Campostella Bridge, 38, 39, 107, 174
Carl D. Colonna (tugboat), 74, 165, 166
Caruso, Enrico, 131
Cassion No. 8, 141
CG-223 (speedboat), 64, 65, 96
CG-228 (speedboat), 67
Charles J. Colonna (fishing vessel), 7, 83
Chas. Colonna—Shipwright, Spar Maker
    and Caulker, 15, 18
Chas. J. Colonna Marine Railway, 16, 18,
    30, 31
Chas. J. Colonna Marine Railways, 16
Chesapeake (diesel tugboat) 55
Chimney Corners (Colonna home), 157,
    172
Christmas Dinner, executive, 154, 158
Christmas Party, employee, 155
Coast and Geodetic Survey, 15, 23, 32, 40
Coast Guard, US, 67, 96, 97, 100, 122,
    137
Collonie (family name), 20
Collony (family name), 20

Index

Collony, Owen, 13, 20

Colonna (family name), 13

Colonna Dry-Dock and Shipbuilding
Company, 16, 18, 52

Colonna Farm, 38, 39, 40, 41, 50

Colonna Marine Railway, 29, 53, 54, 56,
59, 60, 61, 62

Colonna Marine Railway, Corporation,
16, 18, 60, 62

Colonna Yachts, 17, 104, 105, 106, 107

Colonna, Benjamin Allison, 11

Colonna, Benjamin Azariah, 11, 13, 40,
42, 50

Colonna, Benjamin Okeson, Jr., 18, 77,
84

Colonna, Benjamin Okeson, Sr., 18, 74,
75

Colonna, Bruce Cornick, 50, 51

Colonna, Carl Dunston, Jr., 87

Colonna, Carl Dunston, Sr., 47

Colonna, Charles Jones, 6, 10, 14, 17, 18,
21, 22, 28, 41, 42, 50, 51, 77, 126

Colonna, Dorothy Evelyn, 36, 91

Colonna, Edward Holt, 51, 76, 77

Colonna, Eileen Alton, 10

Colonna, Elizabeth Esther, 13, 25

Colonna, Esther Pearl Daughtry, 77, 93,
182

Colonna, Evelyn, 114, 124, 154, 157,
158, 173

Colonna, Fannie Mae, 36, 91

Colonna, Glenn Perry, 64, 77

Colonna, John Owen, 11

Colonna, John Thomas, 13, 15

Colonna, John Watson, 13, 14, 20, 21, 22

Colonna, John Wilkins, 42, 44, 45, 46

Colonna, Karen, 12, 18, 114, 126, 134, 135

Colonna, Major Duncan, 13

Colonna, Margaret Evelyn, 47

Colonna, Margaret Jones, 13, 21

Colonna, Margaret Okeson Dunston, 28,
42, 48, 91

Colonna, Mary Glenn Perry, 76

Colonna, Mildred McClellan, 87

Colonna, Pearl Sykes, 47, 178

Colonna, Rebecca Robb, 13

Colonna, Sarah Boggs, 13

Colonna, Sarah Cornelia, 13

Colonna, Virginia "Jinx" Mansfield, 10

Colonna, Willoughby Warren, III, 126,
134

Colonna, Willoughby Warren, Jr., 17, 18,
19, 56, 77

Colonna, Willoughby Warren, Sr., 18, 19,
56, 77, 90, 91

Colonna's Clipper, 151

Colonna's News, 151

Colonna's Newsletter, 151

Colonna's Shipyard Inc. Company News,
151

Colonna's Shipyard Inc. News, 151

Colonna's Shipyard, Inc., 18, 62

Colony (family name), 20

Constellation (four-masted schooner), 68

Cote, Roger, 157, 160

Cotes, Bob, 123

Courageous (cutter), 96

Crandall Dry Dock Engineers, 98

Crandall, Engineers, Inc., 60

Crandall, James L., 41

Crawfish Jamboree, 152, 153, 154

Crowne Plaza Hotel, 154, 155

Crutchfield, Randall, 18, 126, 135,
136

187

D

Daughtry, George W., 182

Daughtry, Pearle, 182

Dauntless (steam yacht), 104, 105

Defender (racing boat), 87

Delphine (yacht), 104, 105

Diggs, Isaac O., 56

Dipersio, David L., 136

Down River, 17, 111, 121, 136, 140, 143

Doyle, Kristy D., Commander, 114, 115

Drury, W. B., 58, 62, 63

Duncan, R. B., 63

Dupont, E. I., 42

Durable (cutter), 96

E

East Yard, 36, 66, 116, 127

Eastern Shore of Virginia, 9, 13, 14, 20, 126

Edenton, North Carolina, 44, 45, 46

Elizabeth River, 6, 12, 15, 24, 25, 26, 29, 35, 36, 40, 41, 50, 53, 64, 75, 83, 93, 101, 106, 119, 121, 124, 146, 157, 162, 173, 174, 176, 177

Elrod (FFG-55), USS, 113

Elwell, John D., 41

Employee Appreciation Day, 149

Employees of the Year, 151, 152

Essert, Mark, 136

Essert, Martina, 160

Essert, Travis, 160

Evelyn Colonna (tugboat), 74

Executive Dinner Party—2009, 154

F

Fentress, Fannie Cornick, 50, 51

Ferries, Staten Island, 122, 146

Five-masted schooner, 69

Floating Dry Dock, 40, 61, 89, 96, 97, 98, 99, 134, 140

Flow Control Technologies, 17, 110

Forehand, Vernon, 173

Foreman, N. B., 32, 33, 41

Forrest, J. Douglas, 137, 152

Fortify (minesweeper), USS, 94, 95, 143

Four-masted schooner, 68

Fox and Gordon Company, 53

Freedom (LCS 1), USS, 113, 114, 115, 135

Frey, John, 11

Frick (steamboat), 14

Funding, Federal Stimulus, 123

G

Gas-Free-Boat, 66

Gatewood, Rev. Robert, 47, 51, 75, 91

General Harry Taylor (transport vessel), 112

General Hoyt S. Vandenberg (transport vessel), 112, 113

Godfrey, Thomas Walter, Jr., 7, 18, 19, 89, 103, 119, 132, 143, 145

Gordon, Robert H., 41

Graves Marine Facility, W. A., 25

Graves, William A., Jr., 24, 36, 53

Graves, William A., Sr., 15, 24, 26, 36

H

Half Hitch (tugboat), 73, 74, 82, 83

Hardy Estate, 26, 176

Hardy Farm, 32, 35

Hardy heirs, 42

Hardy, Thomas Asbury, 26, 33, 39

Hare, Russell, 163

Index

Harrison, W. T., 41

Hartwig, Chris, 123

Hedrick, Nevin E., Jr., 138

Herbert Plantation, 26

Hodges House, 38, 174, 175

Holtzinger, Manfred W. "Casey," 12, 27, 30, 55, 70, 86, 173

Houseboat and Hunting Lodge, 93, 152, 153, 165, 166, 167, 168, 169, 170, 172

Houseboat Cookout, 153, 154

Hull, W. Vance, 138

I

Iberia (tugboat), 74

Indian River Road, 17, 39, 100, 106, 128, 159, 172, 174, 178

J

J. C. Jr. (tugboat), 74

Jack (tugboat), 74

Jamaica Bay (motor yacht), 106

John F. Kennedy, USS, 133

John W. Brown (Liberty Ship), 108

Jones Marine Railway, L. C., 35

Jones Shipyard, Azariah, 42

Jones, Azariah, 23, 26, 42

Jones, Charles R., 139

Jones, Dolly, 36, 51

Jones, Emmett, 167

Jones, Margaret, 13, 21

K

Kemp, Arrelious W., 172, 173

Kiss the Sky (motor yacht), 139

L

Lady of the Lake (steamer), 16, 28

Lent, Jennifer, 157, 160

Lexington, Virginia, 11, 14

Luciano, Charles "Lucky," 131

M

MacArthur Memorial, 32

Main Yard, 104, 105, 118, 119, 120, 121, 124, 125, 127, 136

Major Mud (mudscow), 74

Maple Avenue, 39

Margaret (barge), 123, 124

Margaret (yacht), 93

Marine Iron Works, 16, 58, 62

Marine Travelift, 89, 119, 121, 136, 142

Markham, Kimberly, 157

Mars, USS, 62, 63

Martinelli, Giovanni, 131

McCoy, Clara Evelyn, 46

McCoy, Henry Francis, 43, 46

Mebane, Kenneth, 139

Medric (fishing vessel), 71

Menhaden Fish Factory, 69, 70

Merritt Chapman and Scott (tugboat), 61

Metzger, Jim, 18

Michigan (tugboat), 74

Mighty Servant 3 (vessel), 97, 98, 99

Monitor (yacht), 138

Morgan, J. O., 176

N

Nandua Creek, 21

Neill, William, 157, 160

New Market, Virginia, 14

Nichols, Bob, 128, 129

Norfolk Barge Company, 17, 74, 82, 99, 100, 134

Norfolk County, 15, 16, 26, 38, 39, 42, 47, 54, 63, 90, 93, 162, 163

Norfolk Diesel, Inc., 151

Norfolk Lighterage Company, 58, 99

Norfolk Ship Salvage, Inc., 73, 74, 82

Norfolk Shipbuilding and Dry dock, 41, 107

Norfolk Towing and Lighterage, Inc., 74, 82, 99

Norfolk, Virginia, 10, 15, 22, 24, 26, 32, 42, 53, 57, 60, 61, 84, 87, 98, 107, 132, 133, 137, 163

Norris, George W., 177

Nowakowski, RADM(Ret.) Mike, 140

Nowland, Anna, 118

O

Oaklette United Methodist Church, 155, 159

Obendorfer, A., 41

Office Buildings, 10, 12, 17, 32, 54, 78, 81, 89, 114, 115, 116, 117, 121, 126

P

Padgett, John D., 18

Paxson. Nicholas Wise, 11

Pennsylvania (steamer), 64

Pennyville, 10, 21, 22

Perry, Mary Glenn, 76

Pescara, 35, 42, 43, 46, 48, 74, 91, 178

Pescara Creek, 17, 84, 99, 115, 119, 127

Peters, Lieutenant Colonel, 173

Pier No. 1, 66

Polaris Ranger 4x4, 120, 121

Poole Engineering, 36, 40

Portlock, Judge William Nathaniel, 16, 54

Powhatan, S/S, 59

Preston, Dean and Mollie, 173

Pungoteague, Virginia, 10, 13, 22

R

Railroad, Norfolk and Southern, 44, 45

Railroad, Norfolk and Western, 32, 35 40, 100, 116

Republic Seabee (company aircraft), 90

Rescue (tugboat), 61

Roanoke (tugboat), 119, 121

Rumrunners, 64

Ryland Institute, 176

S

Saipan (amphibious assault ship), 96

Savannah (barge), 84, 86

Savannah (nuclear-powered commercial ship), 108

Sculpture of Charles Jones Colonna, 126

Sherar, Dr. Nicholas, 21

Ship Carpenter, 6, 15, 22, 23, 25 28, 54, 76, 78, 79, 95, 130

Shipyard Bell, 116, 117, 118

Smith Brothers Shipyard, 10

Sobocinski, Richard, 118, 123, 142

Spriggs, Sandra, 142, 143

St. Paul's Protestant Episcopal Church, 48

Staten Island Ferry/Spirit of America, 122

Steel America, 62, 108, 109, 110, 139, 140, 141

Still, Ricky, 150

Sutton, Charlie, 143

Sykes, Pearl, 47, 178

T

Taft, William Howard, 56, 57, 58

Tarantula (Vanderbilt yacht), 58

Thomas Boatyard, John L., 41

Thomas, John L., 13, 15, 41

Thrasher, Caroline Colonna, 93

Thunderbolt (PC-12), USS, 113
Trade Team, 17, 111
Tucker heirs, 42
Tucker, John, 41
Turkeys, 148, 150

U

US Coast and Geodetic Survey, 15, 23, 32, 40. *See also* Coast and Geodetic Survey
UEB-1 (Navy barge), 96

V

Vandenberg. See *General Hoyt S. Vandenberg*
Vane Brothers, 119, 121
Vess, Lacy, 123
Virginia Dare (motor vessel), 70
Virginia Military Institute, 11, 14
Virus (movie), 112

W

W. W. Colonna (fishing vessel), 70
Walker, Stephen, 143, 144
Wallace, Regina, 125
War Between the States, 6, 13, 14, 21, 25, 28, 47
Ward, Ronald, 18
Washington Point, 29
Watermelons, 148, 149, 181
West Yard, 17, 89, 115, 118, 119, 120, 121, 136, 138, 146
Wheatley, Frank, 146
Wheatley, Sherry, 147
Wilder, Henry Cleveland, 130, 131
Wilder, Joseph Timothy, 130
William A. Graves (sailing vessel), 37
Wilson, Eliza J., 41

Wilson, F., 41
Wm. P. Congdon (diesel tugboat), 55
Wood, W. E., 41
Wright, Ardell S., 147

Y

Yankee (sloop), 28
Yukon (schooner), 38

ABOUT THE AUTHOR

Author and historian Raymond L. Harper is a lifelong resident of South Norfolk, now a part of the city of Chesapeake, Virginia. He first attended the Chesapeake Avenue Methodist Church in 1932 and has been a member for many years. Raymond is a veteran of World War II, having served the US Navy in the Pacific Theater of Operations. He received his formal education from the public schools of South Norfolk, the College of William and Mary, Virginia Polytechnic Institute and State University, Old Dominion University, and Weber State University. He retired from federal service in 1988 after more than thirty-two years.

He served the City of South Norfolk, the City of Chesapeake, and the Commonwealth of Virginia in several capacities, including as president of the Chesapeake Museum Board of Directors, a commissioner on the South Norfolk Revitalization Commission, the City of Chesapeake Fortieth Anniversary Committee, Jamestown 2007 Committee, several committees working with the Chesapeake Economic Development Authority, Reflections Program for the Oscar F. Smith School, the School Improvement Action Team for the Rena B. Wright Primary School, advisor to the Institute for Environmental Negotiations, University of Virginia Graduate School, and on February 10, 2007, he was appointed to the City of Chesapeake Library Board and at this time (2011) is serving in the position of chairman. In 2008, he became a member of the South Norfolk Ruritan Club and in 2011 he was appointed to the Norfolk County Historical Society of Chesapeake Board of Governors. Raymond has had twelve books published and has written numerous newspaper and magazine articles.